MAKE ART WITH PYTHON

Programming
for
creative
people

KIRK KAISER

For Lauretta, for making this happen.

Contents

Introduction Learning to Program with Art and Python

If you want to build a ship, don't drum up the people to gather wood, divide the work, and give orders. Instead, teach them to yearn for the vast and endless sea.
—ANTOINE DE SAINT-EXUPERY, *The Little Prince*

Face it, computers have taken over humanity.

Everyone's face is buried in their phone, oblivious to the world. We've collectively fallen in love with the worlds of the machines.

Because of this, the ability to write new software gives programmers unimaginable power over the collective minds of humanity. Through their programs, they magnify and multiply ideas, which can quickly spread to millions of people in days, weeks, months.

But the process of learning to program computers is treacherous. To the layperson, it seems as if only a mathematically minded people can ever hope to learn to program, and truly control a computer.

And sure, everyone who learns to program must deal with broken code libraries, finding an appropriate programming language, deciding what to make, and so on. There are so many decisions to make along the journey, and so many false starts, that most people give up before they even really begin.

But programming is especially rewarding for the type of people who are drawn to the humanities. They bring a unique perspective and experience to the world of computers we inhabit. They enrich the world of computation by bringing fun and stories and color to our virtual worlds.

And honestly, most great programmers are more like painters than technicians, beginning their software with sketches, tiny little programs that just do one thing, that let them see their ideas before beginning. They'll often make mistakes, write things that don't run properly the first time. Eventually, through sheer force and trial and error, things pushed through to a clear idea.

And writing new programs isn't just for obedient rule followers. Anyone motivated enough can write their own programs, given the proper instruction and patience. Once you understand the fundamental concepts, playing with software becomes an opportunity to play with the flow of thought itself.

This book gives creative, intelligent people with ideas the mental tools to start programming computers and getting their ideas into the world. If you've never thought of yourself as the sort of person who could write a program, this is the book for you.

Almost everyone explores their ideas and shares their creativity through computers now. Why are so few people exploring new ideas with programming?

And why are even less people creating programs that are *fun*?

Why Art

In this book, we'll focus on learning to program through art and the Python programming language.

To an outsider, art and programming couldn't be more different. One seems rigid, with precise instructions that are read by an unyielding machine, and the other is open to interpretation by error prone, emotional humans.

But the process of writing software is the same thing as the process of creating art. In each, we experiment, copy, explore, and then share what we've made. Art and programming are both mediums for exploring our ideas, and then sharing those ideas for other people to play with.

This book, however, isn't about art with a capital "A". We're not making artwork fit for prestigious museums. Instead, this book is more like art with tiny "a", as in arts and crafts, or better yet, finger painting. We're just here to enjoy ourselves, and the act of putting paint on paper. Or in this case, code on the computer.

Step by step, we'll make tiny, understandable changes to the code we've written, and reshape and mix ideas like Legos into new programs.

We'll write programs for drawing, editing photos, and making infinitely repeating shapes.

By manually writing out and running each of these programs, you'll get a feel for how to start exploring and solving problems on your own.

We're just using drawing and art as a medium, because with art we're allowing ourselves to make mistakes and not be perfect.

Why Python

To create our programs, we'll use the open-source Python interpreter.

Open source is a software movement created by a global community of programmers around the world. Each contributes their time and mind to create software, and then gives it away for free.

Each person may contribute just a little bit of a program, but collectively, the resource of open source software is what powers most of the web, from Facebook to Google, to all the servers in between.

Python is a programming language, but also a program that reads and runs programs. Python can load and run programs from files, or you can write code line by line, directly into it. Because Python reads your program line by line, it's called an interpreter.

In this book, we'll use the main Python interpreter, also called Cython.

As an interpreter, Python reads our programs line by line executing each instruction in order from the files we write. Indeed, we can also type out our programs directly into Python, and have our programs run as we type. For a beginner, this makes starting with Python less frustrating, and makes making mistakes less costly.

Python has also been around for a long time, receiving decades of continuous improvements from some of the best programmers in the world. Because of this, it's also got over a hundred thousand "libraries", or programs which extend the capabilities of the Python program itself.

Libraries can connect our Python programs to the internet, write AI, draw images, control 3D printers, direct robots, and more. Each of them just gives us a new set of tools to incorporate to our programs.

Finally, Python is a very easy programming language to read, compared to most languages. At first, looking at Python code might seem confusing, but there are very simple rules for Python code relative to other languages. It uses a lot of white spaces to designate what parts of the code belong to each other. This makes reading other people's code easier, and gives plenty of other, open source code to look at if we get stuck.

The Creative Process of Programming

As you progress through this book, you may encounter some points where you might not really understand what's happening, or why things must be a certain way.

With so much to learn as a new programmer, it can be very intimidating. I've tried to anticipate all the places where you may get tripped up, or not understand fully what's happening.

Maintaining the balance between understanding concepts completely and not understanding them at all can drive you crazy as a beginner.

As we go along, I'll call out the most important parts you should fully understand. Most everything else should be fine to skip over at first. Doing things repeatedly is the only way to really absorb all the ideas of programming.

Keep in mind, whenever we learn something new, our first efforts are often terrible. It can take us hours to type out and run our very first, simple program. The errors we get when we try running things make no sense, and the tiniest things seem to matter in ways they couldn't possibly.

Go easy on yourself if you feel stuck. Just trust the process, that things will get better. Slowly, piece after piece, we begin to find our way. Soon we can successfully manipulate our medium.

The Journey of Becoming A Programmer

By the end of this book, you will be a programmer.

This means you will be able to come up with new ideas, know where to begin after a bit of research, and then maintain the resolve to keep trying until your ideas come to life.

Along the way, if you get lost, it pays to read other people's code. This is one of the most important things you can do when first beginning. Focus on reading other people's code and understanding the ways in which they have approached their own problems.

Initially, you may wonder whether the code you're reading is good or bad. What if you're learning the wrong ideas from "bad code"? Developing a taste for "good code" comes from reading a lot of code, and making the judgement for yourself. Usually it also means writing a lot of bad code yourself. Some people love filing their ideas into classes. Other people like making everything into a function that returns a value.

Part of becoming a programmer is deciding which approach resonates with you. Try a few different approaches out, even if other people call it "bad". You've got to start somewhere.

No "Right Way"

As you progress, you will inevitably worry that you're programming the "wrong way"—as if every program you write is written in the most wrong, convoluted way. You'll want somebody to tell you the right way to write code, and to show you how to organize ideas. But here's a secret: Nobody is coming to save you. Instead, just remember that if you create solutions to your problems, you are doing a good job. If you've learned something new, you're doing a good job.

You may wonder about code that you can maintain, or about code that's fast, but for now, the only important thing is that your code is understandable to yourself. If you can write and read and understand what each line of your code is doing, then you are already a great programmer.

Enough talk, let's begin coding!

A Tutorial Introduction

The only way to learn to program a computer is by writing programs. Rather than beginning with the theory behind everything, we'll jump right in and write our first program. Along the way, we'll pause to understand the tools we're using. But for now, buckle up, because we'll soon write our first program!

Getting Python

You can grab a free copy of Python from Python.org. Make sure you download version 3, as we'll use the Python 3 interpreter throughout this book.

The older version 2.7 of Python is still available, but most of the code we write won't work with that version, so, again, make sure you've downloaded and installed the right version.

After you've downloaded the Python interpreter, you'll need to open and run the program itself.

On Windows platforms, this is easy enough. The Python installer adds a Python interpreter shortcut to your Start menu. We'll want to launch the one labeled "IDLE."

If you're not running Windows, you won't see an icon to run after Python has been installed. This is because the Python interpreter is usually meant to be run from a command line. Windows doesn't really have a full command line just yet, which is why it uses a built-in launcher for Python. For platforms other than Windows, we'll need to use the terminal.

The Terminal: A Program to Control Programs

Have you ever wondered how server rooms work? There are hundreds of computers in a server room, all put together in racks, with network cables running out of them. Not one of these servers has a monitor or a keyboard attached to it. So how is it that they're able to serve up things like Facebook, YouTube, and Snapchat?

These computers are controlled via terminal programs.

The terminal provides a way of running, controlling, and manipulating programs through text only. Instead of using a mouse to control the programs being run, the terminal allows us to send keyboard commands to tell the computer what to run. The programs run in terminals themselves then spit things back out in text.

The Python interpreter is usually run from a terminal. When we're using a terminal locally (as opposed to remotely, on a server connected to the Internet), we call it a command line.

Although entering all your computer's commands through the command line may seem intimidating at first, learning to use the command line well will turn you into a master of computation.

Let's get started with the command line by opening a terminal.

On MacOS, press Command+Space at the same time, and then type in Terminal. This will launch a terminal for you. On Linux, you should have a terminal icon by default.

Once the terminal pops up, you'll be given a prompt. Here you can just type python3 and be greeted by the Python shell. Now we can begin. If you're running Windows, we've just gotten to the point where we can see the shell that you got by opening the IDLE Python program from its icon in the Start menu.

Writing Our First Program

With our Python shell running, we can now begin by typing our first Python program directly into the shell. Each command we type runs immediately. Start by writing the following lines, each followed by a return:

```
import turtle
turtle.down()
```

If you've done the above correctly, a window pops up. In it you'll see a tiny arrow at the center, and in the upper left corner of the window you'll see "Python Turtle Graphics."

Next, we can move our arrow (or turtle) forward, and draw a square. Enter the following commands sequentially, into the Python interpreter:

```
turtle.forward(100)
turtle.right(90)
turtle.forward(100)
turtle.right(90)
turtle.forward(100)
turtle.right(90)
turtle.forward(100)
turtle.right(90)
```

Once entered, we should now see our square in our Python Turtle Graphics window. Hurray!

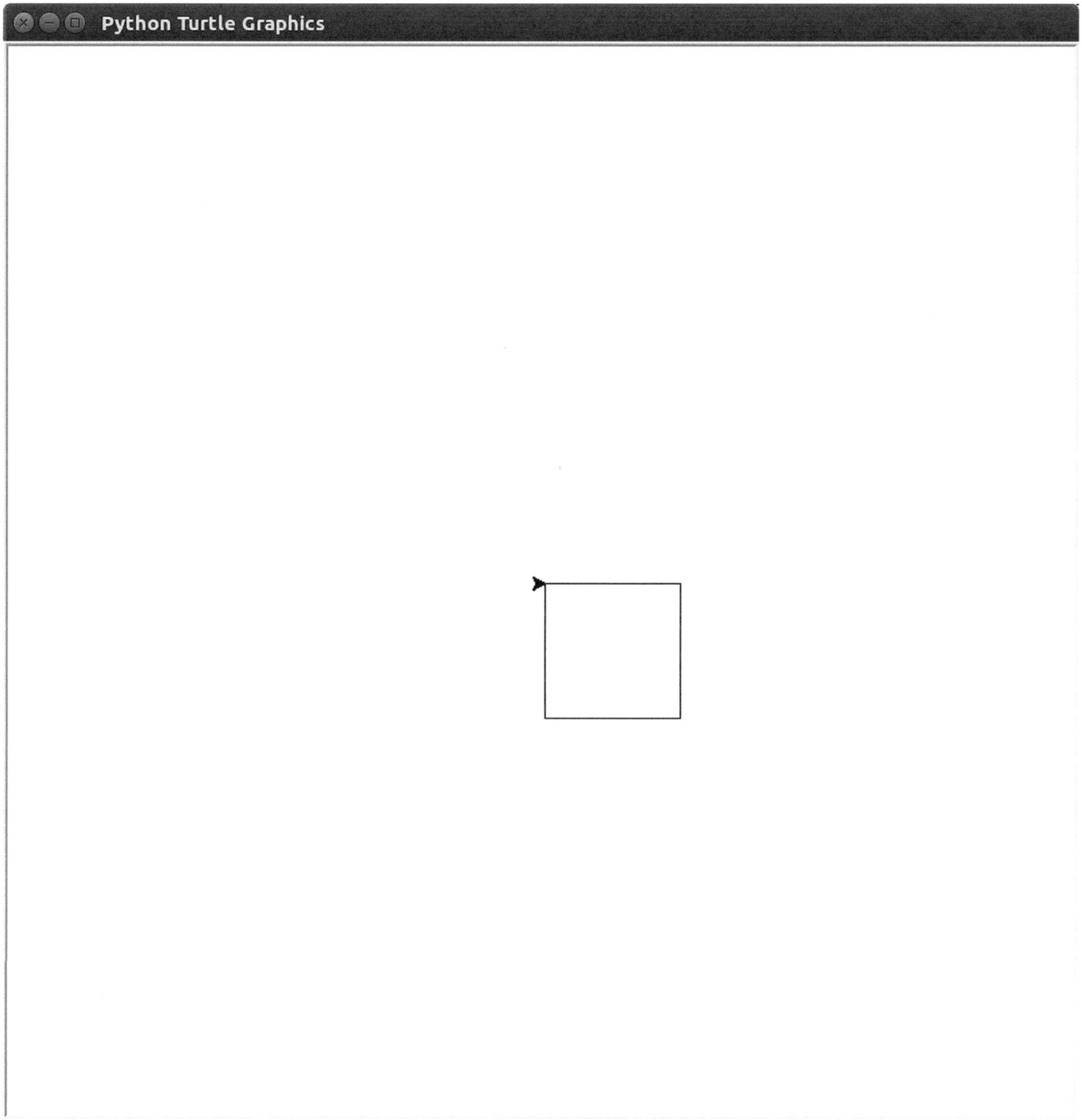

Our first program

Now that you've written something that works, look through the preceding code. Can you make any judgements about it? How would you draw a triangle? Do you remember the rules for a triangle? Three sides, and the sum of the angles must equal 360 to make a full loop. Try changing the preceding values to create three 120-degree turns instead of four 90-degree turns, and see if you can draw an equilateral triangle.

How the Development Cycle Works

Now that we've written a program and played around a bit, what is happening?

When we started by running the Python interpreter, we gave ourselves an environment in which to start typing out Python code and to see it execute right away. When you're trying to solve a problem in Python, it can be helpful to try it out in a shell. Here, we've used the shell to draw using a library called "turtle."

Libraries give Python its power. There are Python libraries for doing nearly everything, from developing artificial intelligence, creating images, or analyzing DNA, to controlling robots.

Normally, our Python programs are written into text files, from an authoring program called an editor. Editors help us write code by letting us know whether we've made a mistake when typing them out and managing our files if we have many of them in our program. The Python interpreter normally loads a set of instructions just like what we've written above from a file. In fact, we can type the above code into a file, and then send it to Python to be run.

The way we tell Python to run the file is by passing its name. It looks something like this:

```
$ python3 myFile.py
```

Let's download an editor and run a Python program like that now.

The Editor: A Place for Writing Programs

Of all things programmers take personally, their choice of an editor in which to write their programs is probably the most important. Each person will have their own reasons for using their editor, and depending on their personality, they may feel very strongly about their choice.

For this book, we'll use a newer editor called Visual Studio Code. It's a free editor developed by Microsoft that comes with some nice Python editing features. Visual Studio Code is available for Windows, macOS, and Linux, so users of each platform will have mostly the same experience writing inside it.

You can download a copy from https://code.visualstudio.com/. Download and install it, and then the first thing we'll do is add the great Python extensions (libraries) we talked about earlier.

Once you've downloaded the Visual Studio Code editor, press Ctrl+e to open the program, and type out ext install python. This will let us write Python code within the editor and see color highlighting and utilize autocomplete for all the libraries we import.

Next, let's create our first Python file. Create a new file from the menu, and then click Save. You'll need to name your file with a ".py" extension. So, your filename could be "first.py" or "firstProgram.py". The ".py" lets the editor know you're writing a Python program and that it should be checking the code you're writing.

Once this is done, Visual Studio Code might bring up a dialog about Pylint not being installed. Click to install it, because this is the Python library used to check our Python code as it's being written.

Finally, we have a place to type out our program. Type out the code from earlier, either your square or your triangle. Then, press Ctrl+' (that's the backtick command), or click View > Integrated Terminal from the Visual Studio Code menu to open the terminal.

Your editor should now look like this:

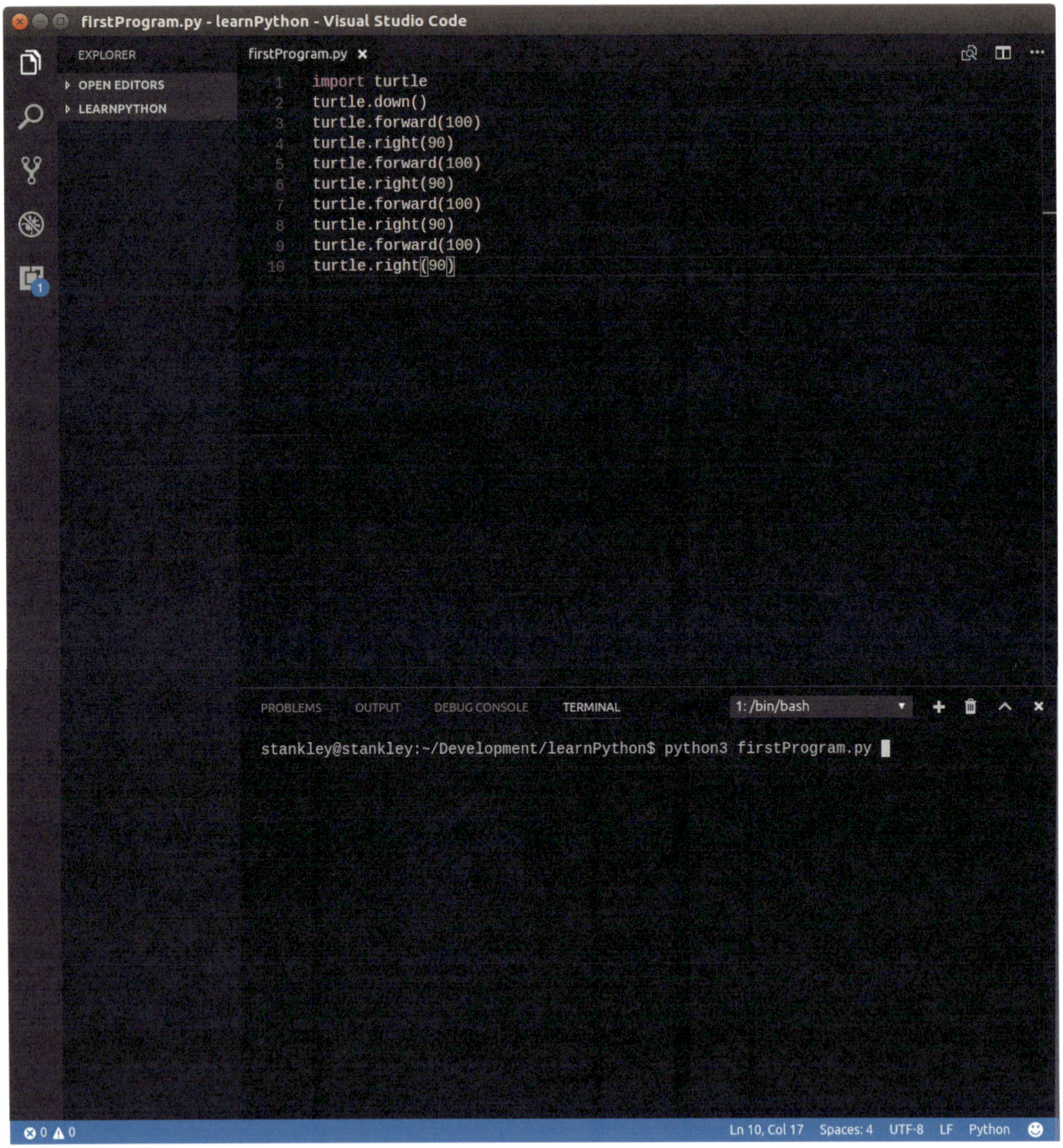

Visual Studio Code

From here, we can run our first saved Python program from the built-in terminal in Visual Studio Code. Type out `python yourfile-name.py`, and you should see your program run.

But wait: Is it just drawing and then immediately disappearing?

The Python interpreter doesn't wait for new commands when it's sent a Python program file. Instead, it reads until the end and then exits. To see what we've drawn, we'll need to make sure the Python interpreter waits.

Luckily, the turtle library has anticipated this need and has added a helper for us. We just need to add a single line at the end of our code, `turtle.done()`, and we'll have a program we can view and close by clicking the Close button on our window.

Congratulations! If you've made it this far, you've written your first program, which technically makes you a programmer. Now that you can draw a square, and hopefully a triangle too, you're ready to take the next step and learn about the tools for building more complicated programs.

We'll stick with the turtle library for now, and use it to see concepts visually.

2
Computational Thinking

Humans can actively interpret and understand what is happening around us. We take vague, incomplete instructions and fill them in using our prior experiences.

For example, we can ask a human to go to the store and buy us a soda. They'll figure out that they'll need some money, they'll need to know where the closest store is, and whether it's within walking distance or if they'll need to drive. They may also figure out that they might need to ask us which type of soda to purchase.

With a computer, however, we'll need to plan and account for everything. And because of the type of programming we'll be doing, called procedural programming, we'll need to make sure we do it all in order.

Luckily, we won't need to create entire worlds from scratch. We won't have to invent what money is, or what roads are, or how to move an arm.

Instead, we can leverage the work of other people, through the world of Python libraries.

As mentioned previously, there are more than a hundred thousand free libraries we can incorporate into our Python programs. Each of these extends the capabilities of Python, saving us work.

For most of this book, we'll use a library meant for creating video games, called Pygame. Pygame gives us a way of drawing to the screen, using shapes and lines and pixels.

But before we jump into using Pygame and getting some real graphics on the screen, we'll need to understand some fundamental concepts of programming.

For now, let's reopen our Python terminal (also called a shell), and import the turtle library so we can start playing with the code.

Remember, the shell is executed on its own, outside of our editor:

```
import turtle
turtle.down()
```

With this code entered, a new Python Turtle Graphics drawing window should pop up, and from here we can start playing with some new programming ideas interactively in the Python shell.

The Loop

Of all the tools of computation, the loop is by far the most exciting, so let's start with it. Loops allow us to tell the computer to do things repeatedly.

When we wrote our first square using the turtle, we ended up writing the same thing over and over a few times. Let's rewrite our first square using a loop, so we can see how loops work in Python.

In the already-open Python terminal, type the following:


```
for side in range(4):
```

Be careful with the last character at the end of the line. That's a colon, which you get by holding down the Shift key on your keyboard and pressing the colon key next to the L key on an English QWERTY keyboard. After you type this out and press Enter, another line will begin, starting with .... We'll need to enter exactly four spaces, and then type out:

```
    turtle.forward(100)
    turtle.right(90)
```

Once you hit Enter, Python will still be waiting for one more return to let it know that the code is finished, and that there are no more pieces of code that belong under the four spaces.

If you entered the code properly, and then pressed Enter twice, your turtle should draw a square all on its own!

But looping a single square isn't really saving us that much work. Let's see the code for drawing a 12-sided polygon instead:

```
for side in range(12):
    turtle.forward(100)
    turtle.right(30)
```

Now we can really save some work!

The Variable

Variables are labels used to name the things we create in our programs.

In Python, you can make up new variables out of thin air, just by creating a unique name, and assigning a value to it. Here are a couple examples:

```
short = 80
long = 100
turtle.forward(short)
turtle.right(90)
turtle.forward(long)
turtle.right(90)
```

The great thing about variables is that they're just labels. This means you can change their meaning later, if you need to:

```
short = 100
long = 80
turtle.forward(short)
turtle.right(90)
turtle.forward(long)
turtle.right(90)
```

One tricky thing about naming variables is that they can't begin with some of the special characters, like dashes, quotes, or numbers. Instead, they must have natural names. If you make a mistake in naming a variable, Python will usually tell you with an error that says something like "invalid syntax".

Another tricky thing is that you shouldn't name your variables after anything that already exists in Python. Your editor should help prevent you from doing this, but it's something to be aware of. Try setting for equal to something in your Python terminal now to see what happens.

However, our variables need not be numbers only. In fact, variables can be words, paragraphs, complete ideas, lists of things, and more. They can represent almost any data type in Python.

Python Data Types

As stated previously, variables are just labels for things. But what are these things?

You've seen one of the types, called an integer. This is just a number without a decimal. We can also save numbers with decimals in Python, and add numbers with or without decimals, and negative and positive numbers too.


```
>>> fun = 10 + 3.14
>>> fun
13.14
>>> fun = fun - -5
>>> fun
18.14
```

Numbers can also be multiplied and divided. Those both work as you'd imagine:

```
>>> fun * 100
1814
>>> fun / 100
0.1814
>>> fun
18.14
```

Remember, if we're not assigning a value to our variable, it's not changed by the multiplication being done to it. Our fun variable should still be equal to 18.14.

We can also set variables to be strings, or groups of words. Let's try that now:

```
>>> fun = 'hey there'
>>> fun
'hey there'
>>> fun = fun + ' cutie'
>>> fun
'hey there cutie'
```

Addition works with strings, but subtraction does not. What happens if we try to add a number to our string?

```
>>> fun + 1
Traceback (most recent call last):
  File "<stdin>", line 1, in <module>
TypeError: must be str, not int
>>>
```

Whoops! Python doesn't let us mix between strings and integers. Instead, we need to convert our integer (**`int`**) into a string (**`str`**) for the line to work:

```
>>> fun + str(1)
'hey there cutie1'
```

Another Python data type, called a list, lets us store anything in a bunch of slots. We can see an example and create one on our own by putting a bunch of things in brackets.

```
>>> fun = ['hey there cutie', 18.14, 0.1814, 18 - 10, True]
>>> fun
['hey there cutie', 18.14, 0.1814, 8, True]
```

As with our strings, we can access each of the things in our list, starting from zero for the first thing, or element.

If you try accessing an element past the length of the list, you'll get an error. Try that now, by entering the following (remember that Python items begin with zero):

```
>>> fun[5]
```

Addition doesn't work with lists, because it would be tricky to know what addition would mean. Instead, we can add new items to lists by using append. We get rid of things inside of lists in two ways: We can pop whatever is at a place in the list and get back that thing, or we can remove the value from the list using remove:

```
>>> fun.append('hi')
>>> fun
['hey there cutie', 18.14, 0.1814, 8, True, 'hi']
>>> fun.remove(18.14)
>>> fun
['hey there cutie', 0.1814, 8, True, 'hi']
>>> fun.pop(0)
'hey there cutie'
>>> fun
[0.1814, 8, True, 'hi']
>>> fun.pop(-1)
[0.1814, 8, True]
```


At the end of the list, we added another data type, called a Boolean value. A Boolean value simply represents True or False. It's a way of saying Yes or No, really. Because it's a data type, you can assign it to a variable.

```
notTrue = True
notFalse = False
```

One tricky thing about `True` and `False` is that they must be capitalized in Python. If you don't capitalize them, they can just be regular old variable names, which can break things in weird ways, when you assume that they should work.

We use Boolean values often when we're trying to decide

between running two distinct parts of our program, or to determine when we should leave a loop. This is called control flow.

Control Flow

How do you get a computer to decide what it should do next? Should it stop, should it loop? Should it skip the next section?

Generally, we use a conditional, or a Boolean value, to represent our decision.

If our user enters square, we draw a square; if our user enters triangle, we draw a triangle.

Boolean logic provides built-in ways to check for conditions in Python.

We can check whether numbers are larger than one another, less than one another, or equal to one another. We can also check whether strings are equal.

The way we ask Python whether two things are equal, instead of assigning the right to the left, is by using two equals in a row, like this: `==`. Here are some examples of other comparisons:

```
>>> 10 > 11
False
>>> 10 < 10
False
>>> 10 < 11
True
>>> 10 == 10
True
>>> 10 = 10
  File "<stdin>", line 1
SyntaxError: can't assign to literal
>>> 'hello' == 'goodbye'
False
>>> a = 'hello'
>>> a
'hello'
```

```
>>> a == 'hello'
True
```

To use this Boolean logic to decide which code to run, we have a few special statements.

We use the if statement to decide whether we should do something. If we want to do something else instead, we use an else statement. If we need to check for other conditions besides our if, we can add an elif before our else statement.

Just as with our loop, each of these statements gets its own white space, with four blank spaces before all the things that belong to it that should be executed.

Speaking of loops, we can use while loops to run the same code over and over while something is `True`.

In addition to Boolean logic, we can also create little blocks of code we can jump to from anywhere, called functions.

Functions get the same four spaces to let the Python interpreter know which code belongs to them. They can receive and return their own variables, depending on what you pass them.

In fact, when we moved our turtle, we were calling functions. These functions were written in the turtle library as bunches of instructions to be executed. They don't return anything, but other functions do.

Don't worry if you don't yet really understand functions or `if` statements. We'll address them more later. Just know that they exist, and that they can return values, or not.

Syntax

The first thing you learn from writing code is how different it is from writing in the English language. This is because programming languages have what's called a formal syntax.

Our formal language, Python, is supposed to be different from our so-called "natural language," because it tries to get rid of any vagueness we might accidentally create with our systems. So, as much as possible, we try to make it very clear what we want our programs to do, exactly, with very specific names, and very specific syntax.

Syntax is the way our lines are formatted, and the way we use our punctuation. In Python, our "whitespaces" are very important, as is our punctuation. If we forget a colon (:), it completely changes what a line means, and can break thousands of other lines of code that are otherwise fine.

Punctuation and spacing must be precise. Coding is not like English, where commas and periods can be used wherever and still convey mostly the same meaning. As an example, each of the indents in Python code must be blocks of exactly four spaces at a time. All lines of code that belong together must use the exact same indentation, or the program won't run at all.

The reason behind this strict spacing rule is to make Python as easy to read as possible. This is one of the core goals of the Python programming language, compared to other languages.

The way we get feedback about when we have broken syntax is through our debugger. It tries running our code, and if something goes wrong, tries to help. The debugger will usually dump out an error message, along with a line number. The line number it dumps out might contain the error within it, or it might be in the preceding line.

Bringing It All Together

Before we jump into writing our first advanced program, let's write one more turtle program that incorporates all the ideas we've addressed in this chapter.

```
import turtle

running = True

while running:
    print('enter triangle, square, or exit:')
    entered = input()

    if entered == 'triangle':
        for i in range(3):
            turtle.forward(100)
            turtle.right(120)

    elif entered == 'square':
        for i in range(4):
            turtle.forward(100)
            turtle.right(90)

    elif entered == 'exit':
        running = False
        print('exiting...')

    else:
        print('not a command')
```


This is a much longer program than our first!

Take your time writing it out, and check very carefully for your quote marks, making sure each one you open is closed properly. Your editor should assist with typing it out, and each of the special commands should be displayed in different colors if you're using Visual Studio Code to type it out.

We've used our else statements here, along with `elif`. `elif` is a way of saying "or else if." We have a while loop, which runs the same thing repeatedly until the thing that follows is False. We let the user enter exit to determine that we've finished.

We also got the user's input from our terminal with the input() function. Because it has the parentheses at the end, this lets Python know input is something that needs to be run. We'll see functions more soon, but for now just know that this means to execute input's code.

When input gets executed, it creates a prompt and then returns what's entered by the user. The input() function is built into Python, so we don't have to import anything before using it.

Once you've got this code running, try adding more shapes. A pentagon has five sides, and each turn is 72 degrees. A hexagon has six sides, and each turn is 60 degrees.

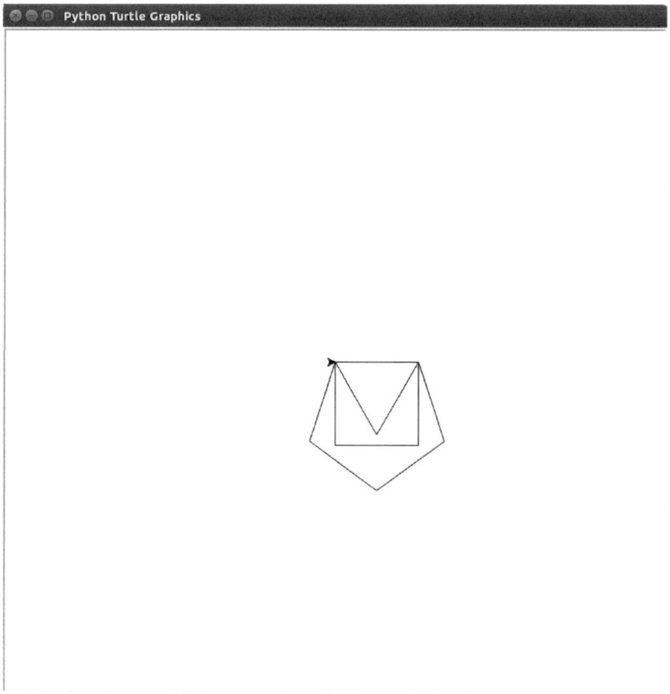

Pentagon, Square and Triangle

Do a search for "Python turtle library." Can you find the function for drawing a circle? Can you add it to the program?

What else can you make?

Writing Our First Graphics Program

Now that we understand the basics of how programming works, let's write a program that does something interesting.

We'll draw a single dot on the screen, called a pixel.

In order to be able to draw directly to the screen, we'll need to use a graphics library, called Pygame.

Before we begin, let's make sure we've got Pygame installed properly. It's easy to do, we just need to type this into a command line:

```
$ pip install pygame
```

Remember, you don't need to type out the dollar sign. That's just a marker for the command line. One you've hit enter, the `pip` program will download the Pygame library on to your computer. You can it installed properly is by typing `python`, and then `import pygame`. If this works, you've got Pygame installed.

Drawing Our First Pixel

Every computer screen is made up of a bunch of tiny dots. If you move your head really close to a screen now, you can see all the dots in a row. These dots are called pixels.

We're going to begin by writing a program to draw just one single pixel.

Start by copying the code written below. If you're reading this book on a computer, you should manually type out the program, rather than copying and pasting. By typing it out, you'll become familiar with the sort of typing errors that can break your programs, and you'll have a chance to practice fixing them by comparing your typed text character-by-character with the code given below.

Remember, even if it takes hours to get your first program running, things will get easier with practice. The initial few programs you write are always difficult to get to work. Just stick with it; every new program you write makes the process faster and better. (Years into my programming career, I can now write programs in just tens of minutes that would have previously taken hours.)

Now let's copy our first program, including all the comments:

```
# first, let Python know we're using pygame
import pygame

# needed to draw pixels
import pygame.gfxdraw

# make sure pygame gets set up
pygame.init()

# Set width and height of our screen we'll make next
screenWidth = 800
screenHeight = 800

# create a screen to draw to with screenWidth and screenHeight
screen = pygame.display.set_mode((screenWidth, screenHeight))

# white is red, green, and blue light in equal amounts
# at maximum brightness (255 for Pygame)
white = (255,255,255)

# black is an absence of light
black = (0,0,0)

# Let's make something so we know when to stop
running = True
```

```python

# Let's run while running is still true
while running:

    # Fill the screen with black
    screen.fill(black)

    # Draw a single white pixel in the middle of the screen
    pygame.gfxdraw.pixel(screen, screenWidth // 2, screenHeight // 2, white)

    for event in pygame.event.get():
        # if you try to quit, let's leave this loop
        if event.type == pygame.QUIT:
            running = False # lets loop finish

    # this is how we update the screen we've been drawing on.
    pygame.display.flip()
```

Once you've successfully copied and run the code above, try running it with the Python interpreter. Remember, you'll need to open a terminal, change into the directory in which you saved the program, and then execute Python with the filename of the program immediately afterwards.

Did it run the first time? If not, look for a line number in the error Python spits back out. You probably made a syntax error, or a simple mistypingtypo. If you get stuck, try looking at the line before or after the one Python throws an error on. Is everything in order?

Once the program runs, it's time to celebrate. There's Aa lot of tricky syntax in just this small amount of code, — includes plenty to trip you up. Getting it to run successfully is a huge accomplishment for a first-time programmer (or even a second-, or third-time programmer!). If your code continues to fails to run, check your code line by line, and character by character, if necessary, comparing it to the code given, until you find your mistake. You can get it; stick with it.

How to Read Our Code

The first few lines tell Python that we'll be using the Pygame library, and also that we'll need the graphics part of Pygame so we can draw just a single pixel.

Then, we create two new things, called `screenWidth` and `screenHeight`, and assign the number 800 to each of them.

These are variables. Variables are used for storing things. As you learned previously, variables just represent what we set them to.

They're called variables because we can change what they mean. On the next line, we could set `screenHeight` to be 600 and `screenWidth` to be 400.

In fact, if your program is working properly, try changing these variables, and see how the program changes. We're just getting started with programming, and part of programming is experimenting to see how things change, like an artist freely experimenting with the colors of paint. Through this experimentation, we learn more about how our programs work.

The screen we create is just a way for us to let Python know what we're drawing on. When we call this function, it calls a bunch of other functions, and Pygame takes care of doing all the setup work needed to create this new window.

Next, we start with our colors. The variables we're creating here are different from those we set for the width and height of our screen. Instead of a single number, they're tuples, with three numbers in them. Each of these numbers represents a Red, Green, and Blue value to make up a specific color. The Red, Green, and Blue values range from 0 to 255. Zero means no color, and 255 means as bright as we can make our color.

Because we're using light to mix our colors, `(0,0,0)` is black, and `(255,255,255)` is white. Again, try playing with these values if you don't understand them. See if you can make your colors red and green.

Finally, we get to our loop. Loops, along with variables and functions, are the most powerful tools in programming. Loops are a way of saying, "Here, do this, over and over, until this happens." In our case, we're saying, "Keep running until the variable running is no longer true."

In this loop, we tell Pygame to fill the screen with black, and then draw a single pixel. Each of these lines of code is calling a function, and each of these functions comes from Pygame. In our case, we're calling functions to start drawing things to our screen.

If you look at the code where we're drawing a single white pixel on the screen (beginning at line 37), you'll see a few weird-looking characters:

```
pygame.gfxdraw.pixel(screen, screenWidth // 2, screenHeight // 2, white)
```

What's going on, exactly?

First, we're calling a function called **`pixel`** from our **`pygame.gfxdraw`** library that we imported earlier.

The parentheses let Python know that we're calling a function, and not looking for a variable. Between the parentheses, we put the variables we are passing in to the function.

The first thing passed in is the variable called screen that we created earlier in the program. We're passing this variable so that the function knows where to draw.

After the screen variable, you see a new expression.

The **`screenWidth // 2`** is something called integer division. It's a way of telling Python to give us only whole-number answers, with no decimal places.

Remember, we have only 0–399 places to draw on our 400-pixel long screen. We can't draw a half pixel, so we must have a number that has no decimal place. The double forward slashes (//) tell Python we're doing that type of division, and the 2 is a way of saying divide it by half.

Finally, we pass in the color in which we want that pixel drawn. Whew, that's a lot to say in a single line!

Now, why are we drawing just one pixel? Because once we know how to draw a single pixel, we can draw anything on the screen. After all, most screens are just made up of a bunch of pixels. Of course, for a 1920 x 1080 HD screen, we're looking at drawing over 2 million pixels. If we want to animate at 30 frames per second, that's over 600 million pixels to specify for a 10-second video!

Fortunately, we usually don't draw to the screen just a single pixel at a time. Instead, we use helper functions and gaming libraries to do the arduous work for us.

Later, we'll write our own function for drawing a line, and eventually end up with a toolkit of new ways to draw on the screen.

Editing Our Code

See if you can find another location to put the pixel. Where do you think the top left, starting pixel would be?

If you guessed 0,0, you'd be right. If you didn't, what did you expect instead? As we get further along in our programming, we'll start to see that ideas like this matter, and that we can change them to work in diverse ways to suit our needs.

If we want to get the bottom-left pixel, what do you think

we'd do? Try changing the program by setting the first and second values to be 0 or the maximum. Which way does it work?

Again, the quicker and more comfortable you become at trying these experiments, the better.

Turning Pixels into a Line with a Loop

Now that we can make a single pixel show up, let's try drawing our first line.

Before we do that, though, can you think of a way to make a line all the way across the screen using our pixel function? If we were to write out all the positions for pixels, we'd be looking at writing 800 separate places to draw our pixels. We'd have to start from `(0,0)`, and then work our way all the way over to `(800,0)`. That's obviously too much work to do by hand. And what if you wanted to change it to be just 10 pixels from the top instead?

Doing things repeatedly is, of course, one of the things that computers are best at. We can use a for loop to make the program draw the line all the way across the screen for us.

The way `for` loops work is by going over every element, one by one. Each time it runs, it moves on to the next element in the list, changing the value of the variable we set. As we saw before, a variable is just a name for holding a value, and that value can change.

We'll use a function called `range()` to generate all the numbers from 0 through 799. It's built in to Python, and we just call it in our loop below. We only need to add a single line to the code we just wrote to make our pixel-drawing program into a whole-screen line program. We'll also need to change the function call to use our new variable:

```python
import pygame
import pygame.gfxdraw

pygame.init()

screenWidth = 800
screenHeight = 800

screen = pygame.display.set_mode((screenWidth, screenHeight))

white = (255,255,255)

black = (0,0,0)

running = True

while running:

    screen.fill(black)

    # Our for loop, for the width of the screen
    for i in range(0, screenWidth):
      # Our pixel draw function uses i to know the current value
      pygame.gfxdraw.pixel(screen, i, screenHeight // 2, white)

    for event in pygame.event.get():
        if event.type == pygame.QUIT:
            running = False

    pygame.display.flip()
```

The first time we run through the for loop, the variable i will be equal to zero. The next time we run through it, i will be equal to one. And so on, over and over until we get to 799. The loop stops just before 800, because we started counting from zero.

Remember that most computer counting starts from zero; not remembering this can make things tricky to understand.

The code in the loop gets executed, over and over again, for each value of i, as i increases from 0 to 799.

Changing Our Line's Direction

If this doesn't make sense to you, try changing your number in the range. By changing your numbers there, you'll get a better feel for how loops work.

Once you get a feel for that, try using `i` for both the x and y coordinates of your pixel drawing. When you do that, your loop should now end up looking like this:

```
# Our for loop, for the width of the screen
for i in range(0, screenWidth):
  # draw the same x and y for the whole width
  pygame.gfxdraw.pixel(screen, i, i, white)
```

What happens? What did you expect to happen?

Since we're working with square screen, for now, we can draw a perfectly diagonal line using this formula. But what happens when you try changing the screenHeight to be something larger?

The diagonal line no longer crosses the screen. That's because we're no longer crossing the whole screen with our values. Drawing a diagonal line from one corner to the other is different for any screen that isn't square. This is important to understand. Just because your code works for one case, doesn't mean it works for everything.

A big part of programming is knowing when your ideas might be wrong before you try them out. A good programmer spends a lot of time thinking of all the ways their plans can go wrong, and makes sure to know if those things matter. As you spend more time programming, you'll begin to get a feel for when your ideas might not work.

For now, though, let's set our screen back to being square, by making screenHeight and screenWidth both equal to 800 for now.

Flipping Our Diagonal Line

Now that we've got our diagonal line, how would we go about making a diagonal line on the other side of the screen?

It might help to try drawing out where you'd begin drawing from, and where you want to end drawing from.

By doing this, we can see that we'd need to start from the very end of the `screenHeight`, and then work our way back down to the zeroth pixel.

If we add a new pixel call where we subtract i from the `screenHeight`, we should go in reverse across the screen. Remember, we only need to change the y position here; we can leave the x position in place:

```
# Our for loop, for the width of the screen
for i in range(0, screenWidth):
  # Our pixel draw function uses i to know the current value
  # drawing a giant 'x' across the screen
  pygame.gfxdraw.pixel(screen, i, i, white)
  pygame.gfxdraw.pixel(screen, i, screenHeight - i, white)
```

By playing around with the code above, you'll get a better feel for how loops work. Try making another loop, to draw more pixels, but instead of using the `screenWidth`, try using the `screenHeight`, and make it vertical.

A Final Challenge

As a last exercise, try making the x we drew on the screen into triangles. Can you make our program look like the image below? If you need a hint, you can add a few lines to our existing code to make it work.

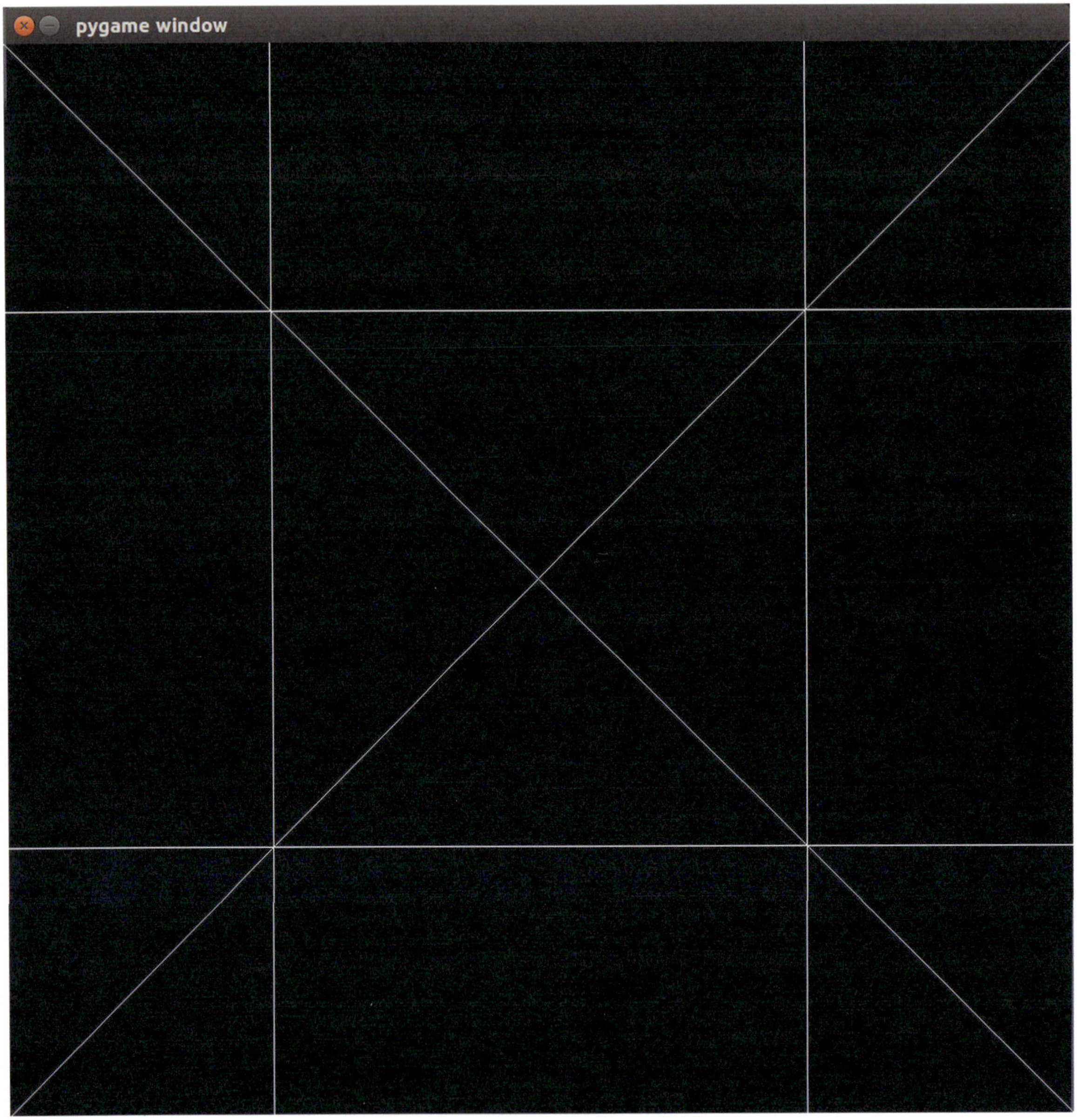

Can you make this shape?

In the next chapter, we'll write our first functions and learn how to create a function that draws a line for us.

Functions Are The Building Blocks of Programs

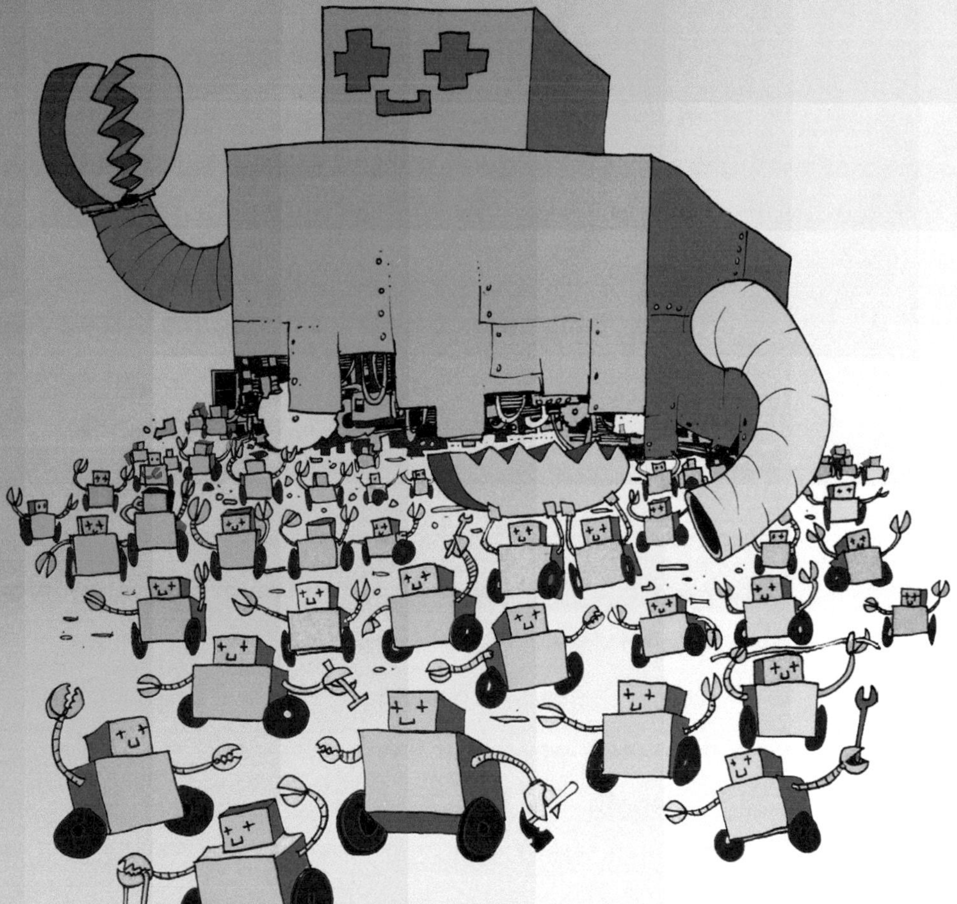

We use functions to link together new ideas.

In the last chapter, we discovered how to turn a loop and a pixel into a line. In this chapter, we'll learn how to turn our loops into complete ideas. We'll write a new function to draw lines anywhere on the screen.

As we progress, keep in mind that the real job of the programmer is to come up with innovative ideas and test them out. After each new function we write, we are given new tools to play with.

From Pixels to Lines, Putting the Fun in Function

So now we can draw a line across the screen, and make it straight or diagonal.

But what if we don't want to make a line in the same place? And what if we wanted to make hundreds of lines? How would you do that?

The first thing we'd do is write a function so that we could draw a line instead of just a pixel. This way, we can put aside thinking about how to make our loops do two things at once.

Let's start by thinking about how we'd want to draw a line on a screen. What sorts of things would we want to know in order to draw any line? What is the bare minimum amount of information we need to draw any horizontal line?

Well, if we're just drawing horizontal lines, we'd really only need to know where our line begins on its x and y coordinates, and its length.

But wait, we'd probably want to know what color the line should be. Oh, and what about thickness? And maybe we don't want to draw from a start point; maybe it's much better to pick a center point and then draw the full length from the center point.

Already our "simple" function to draw a horizontal line is getting complicated—and complicatedness is what stops programs from being written. So, let's start with the most basic form: x and y coordinates from which to start, a length, and a color.

The Mechanics of Writing A Function

Let's look how we create a function in Python:

```
def first_function(thing):
    print('this is a function! you passed in ' + thing)
```

As mentioned previously, two things distinguish creating a function from calling a function. First, we added the def at the beginning of the line, and second, we added the : at the end of the line. Just as with our loop, we'll need four spaces for every line that belongs to the function. When we're done with our function's code, we signify its end by no longer indenting four spaces.

We can call the function we just wrote the same way we call every other function.

```
first_function('hello!')
```

The trickiest part about coming up with writing new functions is making sure they work at all times and in all places. For example, what should happen with our function if we give it a negative number for the x axis? And what if our length is much larger than our screen? Later, you'll start testing your ideas in your head before writing new functions. This way, you'll save yourself the time of writing the wrong thing before you even begin.

But for now, the best approach is to start with the simplest thing when writing a function. After it works for one case, you can try things that might go wrong and see if you can fix them later.

Let’s first just try something we know probably won’t work perfectly:

```
def draw_flat_line(screen, x, y, length, color):
    for i in range(length):
        pygame.gfxdraw.pixel(screen, x + i, y, color)
```

Testing Your Functions as You Go

How do we know where the preceding function doesn't work? Sometimes, it's much easier to test your program by experimenting with possible extremes.

So, what would be an extreme case here?

Well, we could try thinking of lengths that might not work. What would happen if we did zero as a length? What about a negative number for our length? Does that change anything?

What if we send an x and y that are off the screen. Will the program still work? Let’s find out.

```
import pygame
import pygame.gfxdraw

pygame.init()

screenWidth = 800
screenHeight = 800

screen = pygame.display.set_mode((screenWidth, screenHeight))

white = (255,255,255)
black = (0,0,0)

running = True

def draw_flat_line(screen, x1, y1, length, color):
  for x in range(x1, x1 + length):
```

```
        pygame.gfxdraw.pixel(screen, x, y1, color)

def draw_vertical_line(screen, x1, y1, length, color):
    for y in range(y1, y1 + length):
        pygame.gfxdraw.pixel(screen, x1, y, color)

while running: # Let's run until we're not, by looping over and over again
    screen.fill(black) # make the screen the color of your choice

    draw_flat_line(screen, 0, 0, 50, white)
    draw_flat_line(screen, 640, 480, 50, white)
    draw_flat_line(screen, 320, 240, 600, white)
    for event in pygame.event.get():
        if event.type == pygame.QUIT: # if you try to quit, let's leave this loop
            running = False
    pygame.display.flip() # this is how we update the screen we've been drawing on.
```

When you write programs that use a lot of pieces, it can be impossible to think about it all at once. So as much as you can, try to separate out the ways your code works, and make sure each piece works before moving on to the next piece.

Drawing Randomness with Our New Function

Now that we've written our first function, let's write a program to call it thousands of times, with random information. You'll need to edit what you've already got, with the following changes happening to the `while running` loop:

```
import pygame
import pygame.gfxdraw

pygame.init()

screenWidth = 800
screenHeight = 800

screen = pygame.display.set_mode((screenWidth, screenHeight))
```

```
white = (255,255,255)
black = (0,0,0)

running = True

def draw_flat_line(screen, x, y, length, color):
  for i in range(length):
      pygame.gfxdraw.pixel(screen, x + i, y, color)

# Changes to our while running loop begin below

import random # add our random library

while running:
    screen.fill(black)
    for i in range(100): # let's do a hundred lines per frame
       thisX, thisY = (random.randrange(0,screenWidth), random.randrange(0,screenHeight))
        thisLength = random.randrange(0,100)
        draw_flat_line(screen, thisX, thisY, thisLength, white)

    for event in pygame.event.get():
        if event.type == pygame.QUIT: # if you try to quit, let's leave this loop
            running = False
   pygame.display.flip() # this is how we update the screen we've been drawing on.
```

Here's what we get when we add our function and run the code:

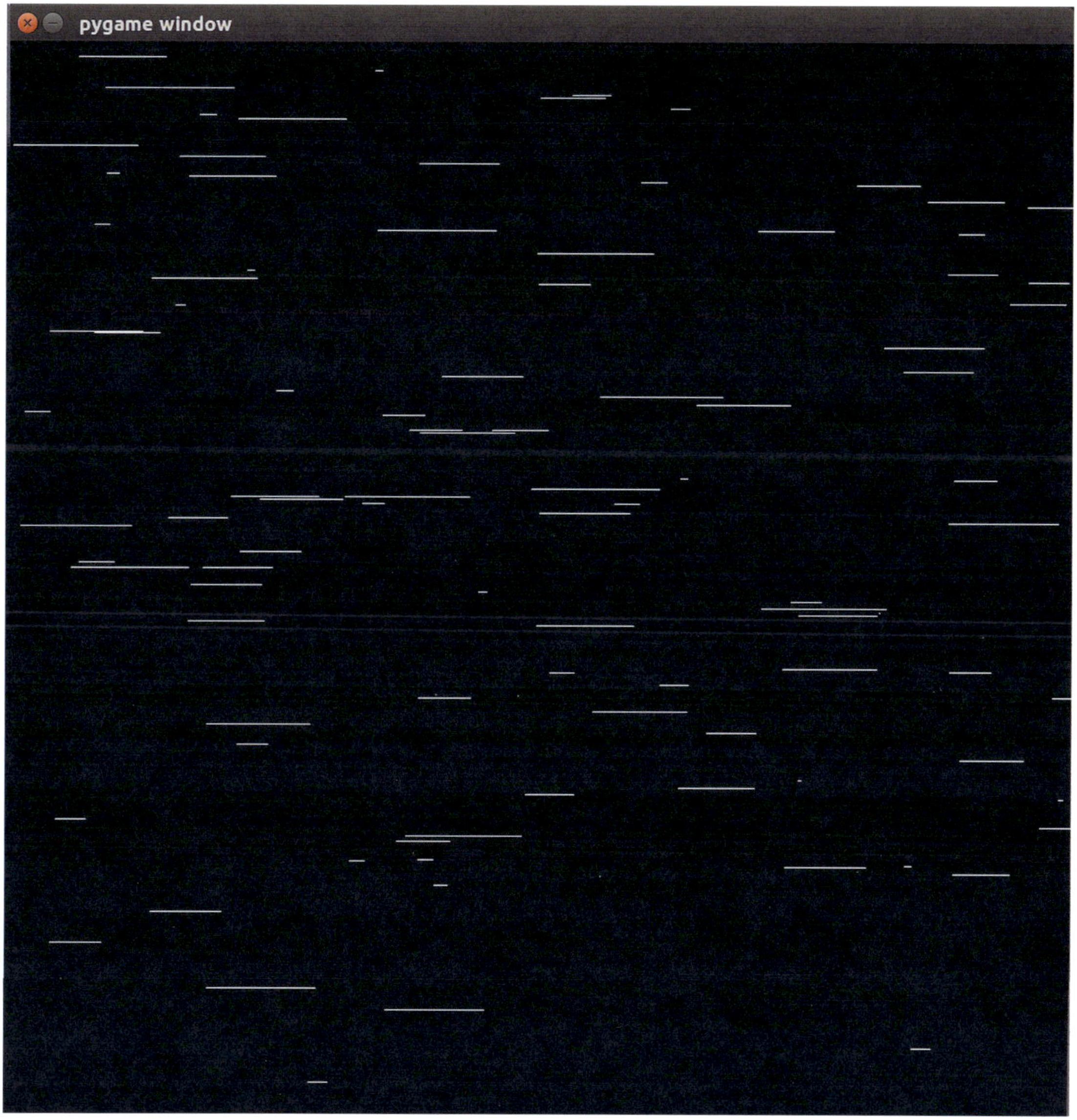

Random Lines

Looks great! We've finally got our first sort of effect, especially when we let it run for a bit and just stare.

Now, let's take a step back. What else can we do with this? We can slightly modify our code, and make a new function that draws vertical lines. All we would have to do is change two lines:

```
def draw_vertical_line(screen, x, y, length, color):
  for i in range(length):
     pygame.gfxdraw.pixel(screen, x, y + i, color)
```

Combining Our Functions for New Effects

Now we can change the function call to the new function's name in our loop, or we can use both at the same time, and see if that makes something more interesting. In fact, let's change the loop from before, and add the `draw_vertical_line`, so we have both functions running right after the other, and see how that looks:

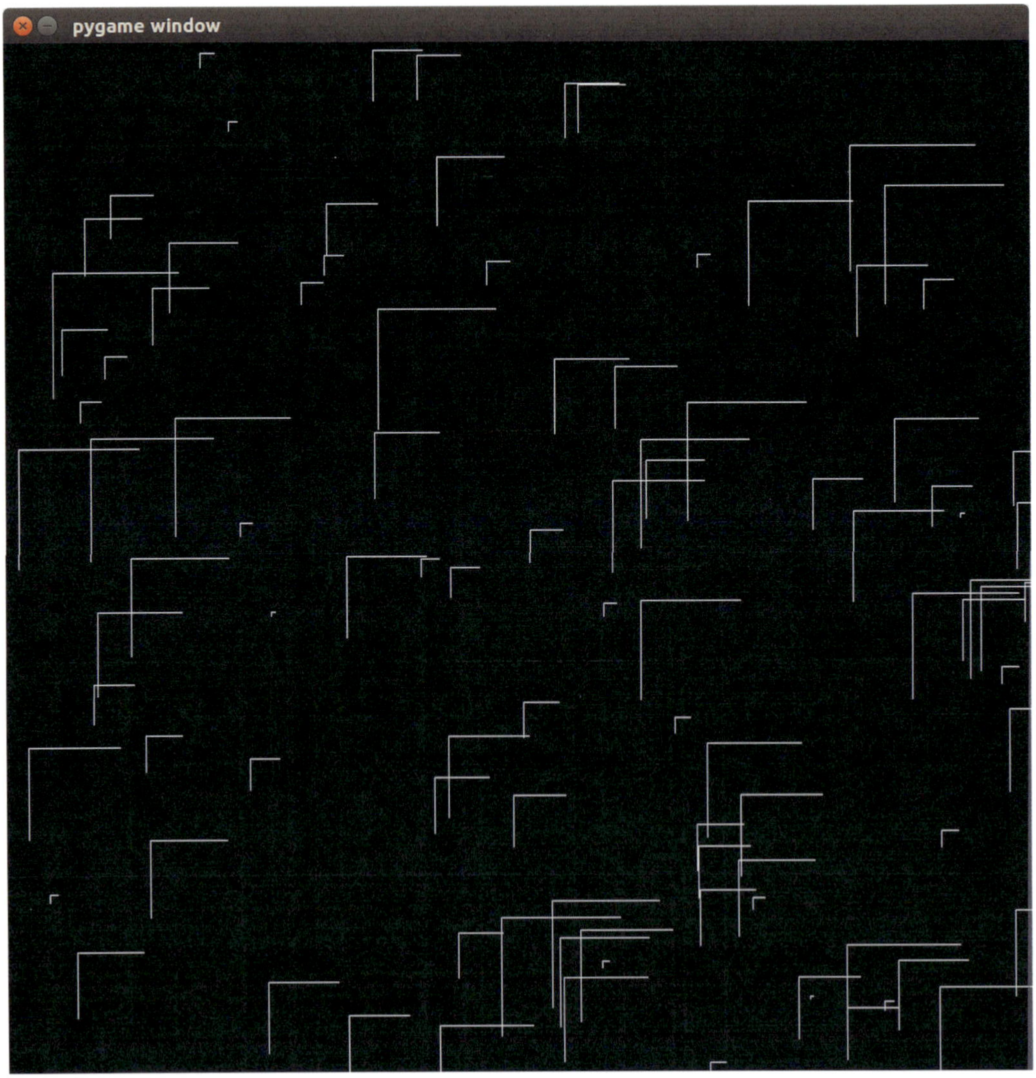

Random Vertical and Horizontal Lines Together

With both functions, what we've really done is create an algorithm. An algorithm is just a fancy way of saying a complete set of instructions for doing something.

The really cool thing about the algorithms we've just built is that they're both stackable. We can combine them and use them in new ways. For each new algorithm we write, we can combine it with others to create entirely new ways of doing and drawing things.

Now, let's go back to our image from above, where we combined the vertical lines and the horizontal lines in the same function. If we'd decided before that our lines should start from a center point, what would the lines look like instead?

5
Reading the User's Mind With Input

"I see you're using the keyboard..."

Do What the Humans Tell You

Having to think before you write a new program is hard. Any chance we get to play with code while it's running provides a chance for solidifying our ideas more quickly.

So far, we've focused on drawing on the screen by writing out all our drawing functions in the program before we run it.

In this chapter, we'll write our first program that we can change while it's running. We'll take the user's keyboard input, and use it to draw a moveable cross hair across the screen. We'll learn how to read from the keyboard, we'll learn what lists are, and we'll learn about if statements.

There will be a lot to digest in this chapter, so take your time and make sure you understand what's happening in each section before you move on to the next part. You're learning something totally new, and it's okay to be challenged here.

Now, let's get to work!

The first thing we'll do is create a new function to draw a "+" sign at any x and y coordinate on the screen. We'll reuse the functions we wrote previously and add only a new call to make sure they're centered on the point:

```
def draw_plus_sign(screen, x, y, size, color):
    draw_flat_line(x - (size // 2), y, size, color)
    draw_vertical_line(x, y - (size // 2), size, color)
```

If you look at the code above, you'll notice that we've got the `// 2` occurring for the vertical and horizontal lines. These lines are letting us get half the length of each line, so we know that our `+` sign is perfectly centered on our x and y coordinates. (And if you remember, the `//` is for integer division; no decimals please!)

When we write the code to draw our cursor, we'll make it so that pressing the up-arrow key moves the x coordinate up by one pixel, and pressing the down-arrow key moves the cursor down by one pixel.

The same things will happen for the left- and right-arrow keys.

Grabbing the User's Input

The way we grab a user's keyboard input in Pygame is with a function called `pygame.key.get_pressed()`. This function returns a "list" of every key on the keyboard, and it lets us know whether every key on the standard keyboard is being pressed.

So, every time you call the function, you get a little snapshot of what's going on with the keyboard.

If you're paying attention, you might be wondering how we know when to check the keyboard. And how many times should we check while our program is running?

Let's write the first cursor drawing program, and see for ourselves in our loop:

```
import pygame
import pygame.gfxdraw

pygame.init()

screenWidth = 800
screenHeight = 800

screen = pygame.display.set_mode((screenWidth, screenHeight))

clock = pygame.time.Clock()

white = (255,255,255)
black = (0,0,0)

running = True
```

```python

def draw_flat_line(screen, x1, y1, length, color):
 for x in range(x1, x1 + length):
   pygame.gfxdraw.pixel(screen, x, y1, color)

def draw_vertical_line(screen, x1, y1, length, color):
 for y in range(y1, y1 + length):
   pygame.gfxdraw.pixel(screen, x1, y, color)

def draw_plus_sign(screen, x, y, size, color):
  draw_flat_line(screen, x - (size // 2), y, size, color)
  draw_vertical_line(screen, x, y - (size // 2), size, color)

# set the start points to the center of the screen
plusX = screenWidth // 2
plusY = screenHeight // 2

while running:
  screen.fill(black)

  # every loop, draw the plus sign again at new position
  draw_plus_sign(screen, plusX, plusY, 15, white)

  # get the list of keys that are pressed / not pressed
  key = pygame.key.get_pressed()

  # check if our key is pressed, change the right value
  if key[pygame.K_UP]:
    plusY = plusY - 1
  elif key[pygame.K_DOWN]:
    plusY = plusY + 1
  if key[pygame.K_LEFT]:
    plusX = plusX - 1
  elif key[pygame.K_RIGHT]:
    plusX = plusX + 1

  for event in pygame.event.get():
    if event.type == pygame.QUIT:
      running = False
  pygame.display.flip()
  clock.tick(90)
```

All right! We can now move our x all the way around the screen, watching it go back and forth.

Each time the loop occurs, and the arrow key is pressed, it adds or subtracts one from the position of our cursor. The loop and the key checking on your keyboard happens so fast that you see this step-by-step update as movement.

But there is a slight problem. Depending on how fast your computer is, the cursor might jump across the screen with the arrow keys, or it might crawl. This is because a faster computer can complete more loops than a slower one.

Pygame has a built-in way of controlling how fast things like this might move, by locking in a set number of frames per second (or updates per second.) This happens with the `clock.tick()` at the end of our program. It slows things down so that the loop might occur only 30 times per second (or whatever else we choose).

Now, in addition to the keyboard checking, we have introduced another bit of logic into our program here: the if statement. It even has a second half you might have noticed, the elif statement.

`If` statements are exactly what we explained before: a way of running instructions only 'if' something is True. In our case, the above code checks to see whether the up arrow is set to `True` in our list of keyboard keys.

When it is, we subtract 1 from the current x position of our cursor. This moves it up our screen by 1 pixel per loop. Immediately after it is an elif statement. This part gets checked only when the if above it is not True. So, we can't press up and down at the same time, and have our arrow go nowhere. Try it out yourself and see. Pressing the down button while pressing the up button always gets overwritten.

You can replace the order of our `K_UP` and `K_DOWN` statements to make the opposite happen. Swap just the values inside of the list, and watch how the first if that is satisfied gets run first. Make sure to update the subtraction and addition to match, and you can change the behavior both ways.

But what do we get back when we call `pygame.key.get_pressed()`?

Unbelievably, it's a list of hundreds of keys on the keyboard. Each key on the keyboard is represented as `True` if it's being pressed and `False` if it isn't pressed. Pygame has mapped almost every key to a place on that list, from 0 to almost 300. Because it's so difficult to remember, for example, that Pygame has established place number 273 as the up-arrow key, the Python developers created another variable we can use called `pygame.K_UP` that represents 273 for us.

Lists Are Lines of Variables, All in A Row

But wait, what's a list? As we saw in chapter two, it's only a counted list of similar things. We can add items to it or subtract items from it, and we can count how many things are included.

Each "slot" in a list is accessible by its associated *key*. A key is just a way of designating which slot to pick. For all lists, we start counting at zero. So, the first item in our list is `0`. We access that element using square brackets.

There's also a cool trick for accessing the last element in a Python list without having to know how long the list is. You do this by writing `[-1]` at the end of your list.

Those brackets are how you tell Python that you're trying to access one of the things inside of your list.

Is this confusing? Is this too much? Let's create a list of cursors next, and see if that helps.

Creating a List, Adding Things to Your List

Let's create a method of drawing using our cursor and lists. We'll make it such that pressing the space bar draws a cursor wherever the cursor is positioned. We can keep track of all the x and y coordinates we've placed by storing a list of every coordinate.

The way we'll do this is somewhat tricky though. Because we'll need both an x and a y coordinate for each element, our list will be filled with lists! This means we'll set `[0]` to be our x, and `[1]` to be our y for all the cursor positions we add to our list.

If this is terribly confusing, looking at the code should help. See how we create and add each of these new lists to our drawing, and then how we pull out each of these x and y coordinates from the list:


```
# Add a new list before our loop starts
# Otherwise, the list gets forgotten every
# time the loop completes
cursorList = []

while running:
    screen.fill(black)

    draw_plus_sign(screen, plusX, plusY, 15, white)

    # loop over each of our cursor positions. if empty, skips
    for plusSign in cursorList:
      draw_plus_sign(screen, plusSign[0], plusSign[1], 10, white)

    key = pygame.key.get_pressed()

    # add our new check for the SPACEBAR
    if key[pygame.K_SPACE]:
        # take the current position of the cursor
        # and create a list holding x and y
        newPlace = [plusX, plusY]
```

```
# add that list to our cursorList
cursorList.append(newPlace)
```

Replace your previous while running loop with the above. Make sure you create the cursorList variable outside of the while running: loop; otherwise, it will reset to empty for every loop.

You should now have a completely new way to draw on the screen, and hopefully you now understand a bit more about how lists work.

Again, we're creating a list of lists, so in our for loop, we're taking each position in our list and assigning its value to the plus-Sign variable. We then take the first element, `[0]`, from this list, and then the second element, `[1]`, and send them off to be drawn by our previous `draw_plus_sign` function.

Adding the new key check for our space bar is easy enough, and looks just like our previous key checking. We create our list of our current cursor position using the same setup as before. We just use the brackets to let Python know they should be in a new list.

And, above, where we create the first cursorList, we're letting Python know that we expect it to be a list. We do this so when it's empty we can do a `.append()` to the list, to have things added. If we didn't do this, Python wouldn't be able to append to a variable it doesn't know about.

You might notice in running this program that holding down the space bar lets you draw a fairly solid line with the cursor. For example, I can make an interesting design by holding down the arrow keys in diagonal directions:

The Mona Lista

As an experiment, can you add a new key to change the color of the cursor you're using to draw?

If you're stuck on ideas for color, here are a few colors you can try:

```
red = (255,0,0) # red is the first value, 255 is max
green = (0,255,0) # green is the second value
blue = (0,0,255) # blue is the last
grey = (125,125,125) # half way to all the maximums
```

You can experiment by mixing the values for each of the colors. Just remember that they're all in Red, Green, Blue format.

6
More Playing with Loops

The Never Ending Loop

Drawing with Our New Cursor

We've seen how loops allow us to run code repeatedly. Because repeating code is so important in programming, we'll spend extra time here to really make sure we understand what's happening.

Drawing with Our New Cursor

In skateboarding, the most fundamental trick is the ollie. Mastering the ollie is essential to developing as a skateboarder, as it is the trick through which all other tricks become possible.

But without fail, every beginning skateboarder wants to skip learning the ollie well. Instead, after landing a single ollie they'll want to get right into the most advanced tricks: the kickflips or 360 flips or 180s.

Months later, they still can't do anything well.

Without a good ollie as your foundation, you can't grind or kickflip, and everything else you try to do becomes more difficult. Loops are the ollies of programming. They'll show up everywhere, and most problem solving will involve some sort of loop. Because they're so important, we're going spend another chapter on them.

In the last chapter, we figured out a way to use loops to draw all over the screen. But our drawing capabilities were rather bland. The cursor retained the same shape and color throughout the entire drawing process.

Looping a Fade

For a first trick, let's try making our draw loop fade from black to white.

To do that, we need to keep track of where we are in the list, and how many cursors we've drawn. We also need a way to make sure we don't go above 255 for any of our color values.

We could start by keeping track of how many cursors we've drawn in our loop.

In Python, there's a function to return the count of each thing as we go through a list, plus the value at each place. This function is called `enumerate`.

`enumerate` will return each item in our list, along with its place. But after we reach 255, how do we start back over at zero, and then begin increasing all over again?

We could use the *division remainder* of 255 to cycle through each of the 255 values. This is represented in Python with the percent (`%`) sign.

The division remainder is just like what you learned in middle school. Instead of returning a decimal for uneven fractions, it returns the "remainder" left over from a division of two numbers.

Let's see how it works, by opening another Python shell.

```
>>> 5 % 4 # the remainder of 5 divided by 4
1
>>> 17 % 4 # the remainder of 17 divided by 4
1
>>> 25 % 5 # the remainder of 5 divided by 5
0
```

Getting the remainder of a number allows us to split up our repetition into chunks. We can run through hundreds, or thousands, of numbers, and get the same looping numbers over and over, as our remainder repeats.

If you still don't understand the division remainder, try playing with some test numbers in a Python interpreter shell. Try adding another number to the number you're adding into your modulus to see it count.

Better yet, let's visualize the looping of the modulus operator by changing our previous code.

Replace the drawing loop from the previous chapter, replacing only where we iterate over each of the items in the cursorList. So, the for item in cursorList for loop should be replaced with the following.

We'll change the `draw_plus_sign` code and use the % operator to remain below 255, using the enumerate function to count over each item in the list, like this:

```
for i, plusSign in enumerate(cursorList):
    draw_plus_sign(screen, plusSign[0], plusSign[1], 10, (i % 255, i % 255,
        i % 255))
```

When we draw using this new code, our cursor looks something like this:

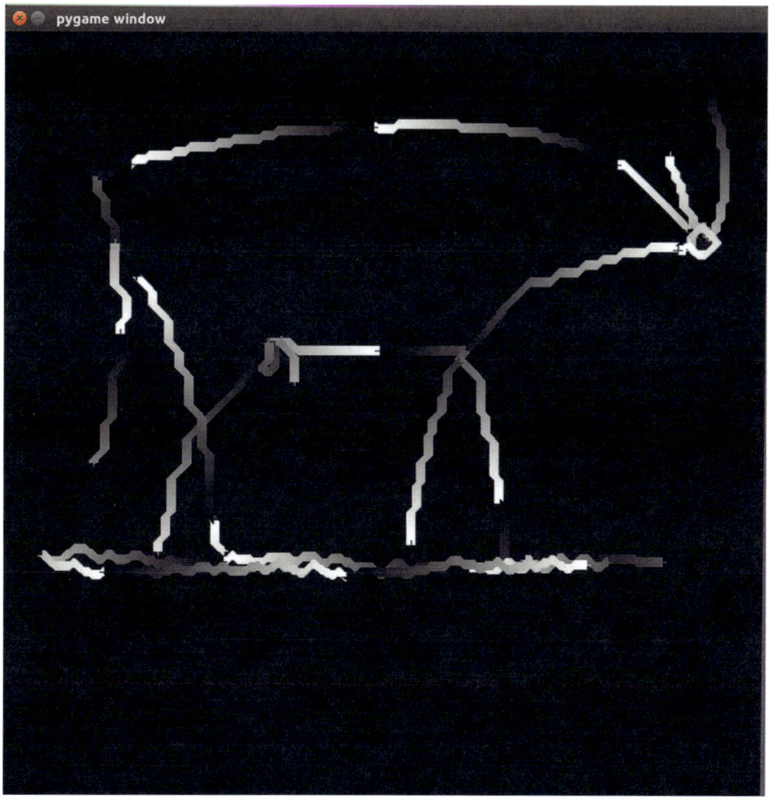

The Faded Line Bull

The enumerate function again returns two values for our loop:the current item and the count of how many items we have so far.

By doing a modulus of our current number by 255, we count to 255 over and over again, even as we have thousands of items in our cursorList.

With this, we've really got something that's starting to look interesting. Because of the fading, the drawing almost looks 3D.

But wait. It's currently drawn with solid white (at its brightest) bouncing right back to solid black. How would we make it so that everything was softer and transitioned gradually, from white to black and then back to white in the opposite direction?

For that, we'd use the sine function.

Making Our Fade into a Wave

The sine wave function creates a perfectly curvy wave.

You send it numbers from -infinity to +infinity, and for each step it generates the same number, consistently going up and down, repeatedly.

It's like the `%` function in that it never goes out of its bounds, -1 to +1, over and over again.

To use it, we'll add another import at the top of our file, for math. Then, after we've imported math, we can call it from within our drawing function.

Again, the sine function goes from -1 to 1, repeatedly. So, to draw from black to white, that means when we're at 1 we should be at 255, and when we're at -1 we should be at 0. This is super tricky, and it's worth taking a minute to think about.

If you get stuck trying to understand this, try playing with the numbers below after you've got the program running. It should make more sense after some trial and effort. Here I'll copy out our whole program again, even though we should just be changing a few lines.

I've added this here in case you've gotten stuck or lost after trying to change the previous lines

```
import pygame
import pygame.gfxdraw

import math
pygame.init()

screenWidth = 800
screenHeight = 800

screen = pygame.display.set_mode((screenWidth, screenHeight))
clock = pygame.time.Clock()

white = (255,255,255)
black = (0,0,0)

running = True

plusX = screenWidth // 2
plusY = screenHeight // 2

def draw_flat_line(screen, x1, y1, length, color):
  for x in range(x1, x1 + length):
      pygame.gfxdraw.pixel(screen, x, y1, color)

def draw_vertical_line(screen, x1, y1, length, color):
  for y in range(y1, y1 + length):
      pygame.gfxdraw.pixel(screen, x1, y, color)

def draw_plus_sign(screen, x, y, size, color):
    draw_flat_line(screen, x - (size // 2), y, size, color)
    draw_vertical_line(screen, x, y - (size // 2), size, color)

centerPoint = (screenWidth // 2,  screenHeight // 2)

# Add a new list before our loop starts
cursorList = []
```

```
while running:
    screen.fill(black)

    draw_plus_sign(screen, plusX, plusY, 15, white)

    # loop over each of our cursor positions. if empty, skips
    for i, plusSign in enumerate(cursorList):
      rI = math.sin(i * .01) * 127 + 128
      draw_plus_sign(screen, plusSign[0], plusSign[1], 10, (rI, rI, rI))

    key = pygame.key.get_pressed()
    if key[pygame.K_SPACE]:
        newPlace = [plusX, plusY]
        cursorList.append(newPlace)

    if key[pygame.K_UP]:
        plusY = plusY - 1
    elif key[pygame.K_DOWN]:
        plusY = plusY + 1
    if key[pygame.K_LEFT]:
        plusX = plusX - 1
    elif key[pygame.K_RIGHT]:
        plusX = plusX + 1
    for event in pygame.event.get():
        if event.type == pygame.QUIT: # if you try to quit, let's leave this loop
            running = False
    pygame.display.flip() # this is how we update the screen we've been drawing on.
```

We've got our very first, correctly bouncing sine wave. And yep, it really looks like we've finally got our perfectly flowing gradients:

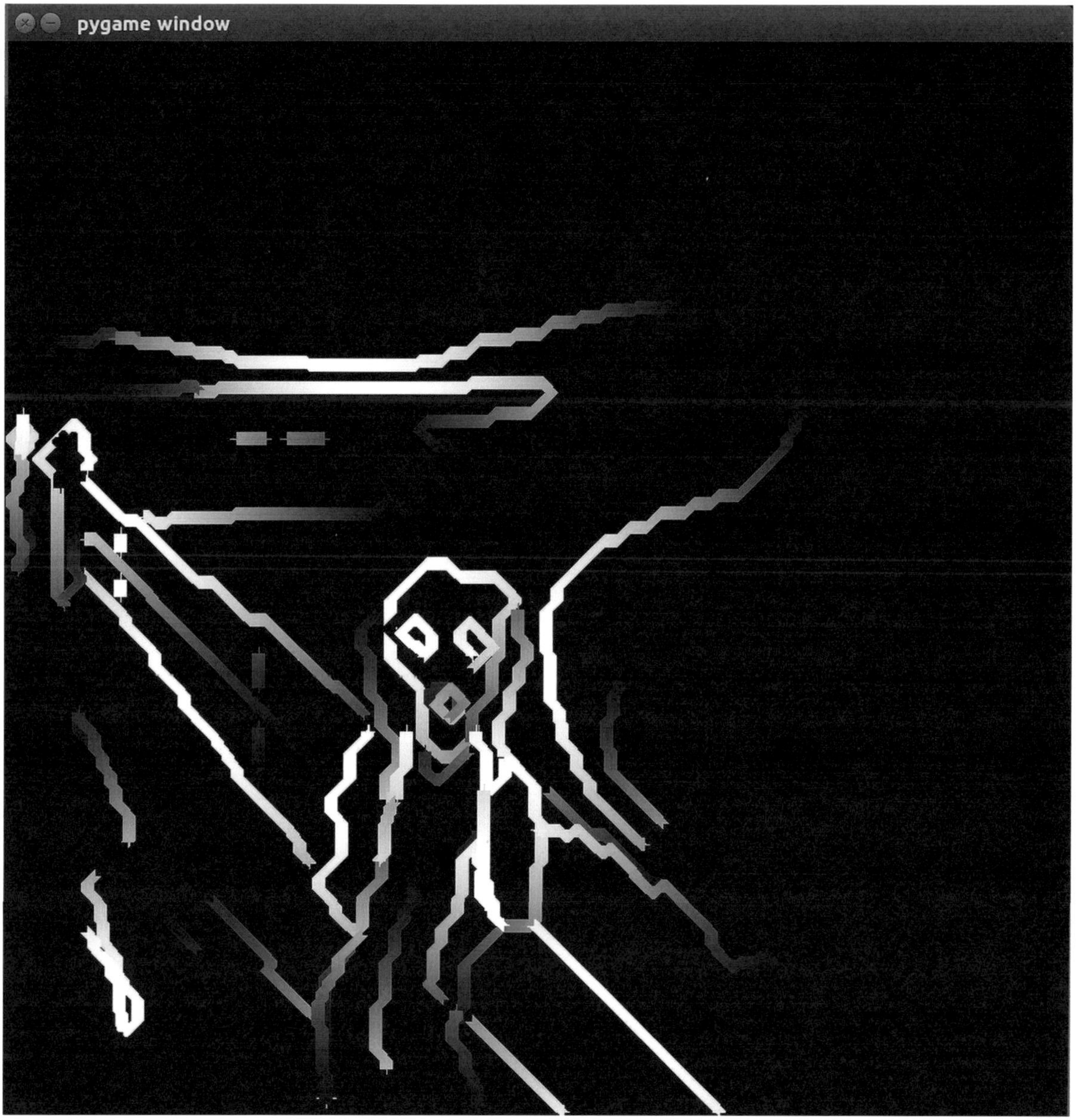

Sine Wave Scream

But wait, what's going on in that math.sin() function line? Why are we multiplying by 127, and why are we adding 128? And why are we multiplying i * .01?

Let's take it apart.

The sine wave function takes in any number and returns a number between -1 and 1. -1 * 127 is -127, + 128 is 1. So, we start from the darkest of blacks, and then 1 * 127 + 128 is 255, so we go to the strongest value for white.

But why are we multiplying i * .01? Try changing it to .05. What happens? Try changing it to 1. Does it do what you expected?

Multiplying by .01 lets us set the "frequency" of our sine wave. We multiply by smaller numbers to make longer waves, and by larger numbers to make the waves of color smaller.

Fading Colors to Make Rainbows

The coolest thing we can do with our sine wave, though, is to use one for our red, green, and blue colors. If we give each a slight different starting point, their cycling generates a rainbow.

Just like before, we only need to replace the part of our code where we draw the `cursorList` itself. Change the loop from the code above to the following:


```
for i, plusSign in enumerate(cursorList):
  rR = math.sin(i * .01) * 127 + 128
  rG = math.sin(i * .01 + 5) * 127 + 128
  rB = math.sin(i * .01 + 10) * 127 + 128
  draw_plus_sign(screen, plusSign[0], plusSign[1], 10, (rR, rG, rB))
```

When we run the above code, each sine wave is just a bit out of sync with another. Each of these colors is going through their own rotation, which generates the rainbow colors together. Try changing how out of sync they are with one another to experiment more with color rotation.

Now, let's make one final move, and make our colors increase and decrease in brightness, just like our white-to-black did before.

Can you see how to make this happen?

If we create a sine function that returns numbers from 0 to 1, we could multiply our chosen color by that number, and make it more or less dark, without going above or below our existing 0 to 255 color choice.

So, how do we turn a function that returns numbers from -1 to 1 into a function that returns numbers from 0 to 1?

First, we add 1 to our result, so our numbers are from 0 to 2. Then, we divide by 2, and we have our numbers ranging from 0 to 1.

Once we've got our multiple set up properly, we just multiply each of our chosen colors by that fade to get our final color. Here's what the code looks like:

```
for i, plusSign in enumerate(cursorList):
      rR = math.sin(i * .01) * 127 + 128
      rG = math.sin(i * .01 + 5) * 127 + 128
      rB = math.sin(i * .01 + 10) * 127 + 128

      # Generate a separate fader for all of them to be scaled by
      # Remember, we need from 0 - 1, not -1 to 1, hence the add
      # and divide.
      fader = (math.sin(i * .1) + 1) / 2
      rR = rR * fader
      rG = rG * fader
      rB = rB * fader
      draw_plus_sign(screen, plusSign[0], plusSign[1], 10, (rR, rG, rB))
```

The result is that we have one more way in which our colors keep fading, both in and out of full brightness, and returning to total black.

What do you think of the way we've created these color changes? Do you see a new way our drawing could be improved? Maybe something else we could oscillate?

We could also change the size of our cursor, to match everything else. Let's try that now, and see if that gives us another interesting effect.

```
# loop over each of our cursor positions. if empty, skips
    for i, plusSign in enumerate(cursorList):
        rR = math.sin(i * .01) * 127 + 128
        rG = math.sin(i * .01 + 5) * 127 + 128
        rB = math.sin(i * .01 + 10) * 127 + 128
        # Generate a separate fader for all of them to be scaled by
        # Remember, we need from 0 - 1, not -1 to 1, hence the add
        # and divide.
        fader = (math.sin(i * .02) + 1) / 2
        rR = rR * fader
        rG = rG * fader
        rB = rB * fader

        # try changing the value below from .005 - 5.2
        # you'll get some interesting results in between
        sizer = int(math.sin(i * .043) * 35 + 35)
        draw_plus_sign(screen, plusSign[0], plusSign[1], sizer, (rR, rG, rB))
```


Now we've really got some interesting ways of drawing. And we've only added three things to change when we move our cursor.

By changing the size of our last multiple in the sine wave, we can generate different ways of building and drawing our lines of cursors. We go from having a solid line to having feathers, to having grids, and all the way back down to having long, growing lines.

But these colors are just begging to be taken further—asking to be made to repeat themselves. Let's try that now:

```
while True:
    # after our cursor position loop insert the following:

    # First we take top left quarter of screen, make a copy
    cropped = pygame.Surface((screenWidth // 2, screenHeight // 2))
    cropped.blit(screen, (0,0), pygame.Rect(0, 0, screenWidth // 2,
       screenHeight // 2))

    # flip that copy on just the y axis, paste below
    belowFlipped = pygame.transform.flip(cropped, False, True)
    screen.blit(belowFlipped, pygame.Rect(0,screenHeight // 2,
       screenWidth // 2, screenHeight))
```

```
# flip original copy on just x axis, paste to the right
topRight = pygame.transform.flip(cropped, True, False)
screen.blit(topRight, pygame.Rect(screenWidth // 2, 0, screenWidth,
  screenHeight // 2))

# finally flip both axis, paste bottom right
bottomRight = pygame.transform.flip(cropped, True, True)
screen.blit(bottomRight, pygame.Rect(screenWidth // 2, screenHeight // 2,
  screenWidth, screenHeight))
# ... code from below continues
```

With this, we cut down the size of our drawing area, but flip and mirror it across multiple windows.

We do this by creating a new surface to draw on, and then blit, or copy over, the image to this screen. Our cropped.blit line of code is how we copy over this original square, and from there we rotate and flip as appropriate for each corner of the screen.

Again, try playing with these flips to see if you can create something new.

More Experimenting

With this final change, we can see the potential of having just a few variables to tweak. We're limited only by our experimentation and imagination. A few values changed can create weird ways of drawing:

Mirror Fade Size Effects

In the next chapter, we'll learn how to program using input from the mouse to make creating artwork even easier.

Inventing Ideas with Classes

Drawing in New Ways

Our first drawings worked with lists of lists, with each list storing an x and y position of the cursor. We used the space bar to create multiple cursors and produce the illusion of a continuous line.

When we wanted to draw our cursor in diverse ways, we just changed the loop that drew our list.

Using our current approach, how could we add several types of lines at the same time, so that we create lines of various changing widths, straight lines, and curving rainbow lines all in the same drawing? Could we make that happen with our lists of lists?

On first thought, we could add a new list, with one list for each line. Then, we'd have a list of lists of lists, and things would get even more complicated. But what if we wanted lines of diverse colors in each of those lines?

We'd have lists of lists of lists, with each one having their own x, y, Red, Green, and Blue values. All this adds up quickly, and gets difficult to talk about, or even think about.

This lists approach just isn't very flexible. It becomes hard to reason and make changes. Remember that part of being a good programmer is making it easy to alter your code.

Making Your Ideas Part of the Language

If reading and updating lists of lists of lists is so confusing, how is it that programmers can keep track of so much information on the screen at once?

When playing video games, we can see hundreds of enemies on the screen at times, and each must have its own lengthy list of properties.

Where is all this information? Programmers hide away the information with classes.

Classes let us think directly about the problem we're trying to solve. Instead of thinking about the type and shape of the information we're accessing, we create names for each property of the thing.

For example, with our previous programs we might instead create a Line class, rather than keep track of our line with lists.

And in that line class we might have a list of x and y start and stop points, and a color for the line. Using this class, we can access each property from within the object itself.

With classes, we have fewer layers of stuff to think about. And the less we think about all the layers of stuff we've built, the more mental attention we can apply to solving the problem at hand.

Creating Our Line Class

Let's look at what a Line class might look like in Python:

```
class Line():
    def __init__(self):
        self.linePoints = []

    def __repr__(self):
        if not self.is_line():
            return "Not a line yet."

        return "Line from %s to %s" % (self.linePoints[0],
             self.linePoints[-1])

    def is_line(self):
        if len(self.linePoints) > 1:
            return True
        return False

    def add_linepoint(self, x, y):
        self.linePoints.append((x, y))
```

```
a = Line()

# Prints "Not a line yet."
print(a)

a.add_linepoint(1,2)
# Prints "Not a line yet"
print(a)

a.add_linepoint(3,5)
# Prints "Line from (1, 2) to (3, 5)
print(a)

a.add_linepoint(6,1)
# Prints "Line from (1, 2) to (6, 1)
print(a)
```

There are a few new ideas here, and a few things to look out for.

First, we let Python know we're defining a class by putting the keyword `class` before the name of our class.

Next, after the name `Line`, we use the parentheses, just as with a function.

After defining the class, we define two very different looking functions.

The first, called `__init__` is a special function. `__init__` always takes a very special variable first, called `self`. `self` is exactly what you might think it is: the class itself.

The function `__init__` exists for every class in Python. These `__init__` functions tell Python what to do when the object is first made, or initialized.

In our case, we've told Python to create our list where we'll keep all our points in our line. We won't put any points in our line just yet; we'll add them later.

After this is another special function, called `__repr__`. This is what Python uses to represent the object when printed to the console. We've made it so Python will print out the start and end points to which the line is set through the command line.

Both special functions, `__init__` and `__repr__` begin and end with double underscores. These double underscores are a way of accessing built in methods in Python. By defining our own here, we're overwriting the built in ones in Python.

After our special functions, we have two regular functions that let us check on our object instance. Because they belong to the class itself, these functions won't be available to call outside of the object instances themselves.

First, we have `is_line`, which we can use to check to see whether we have at least two points to compose a line in our object.

Finally, we include a way of adding points to our line, using the `add_linepoint` function.

Planning Your Class Design

Classes can be especially tricky for beginners, because it's often difficult to know when you should use them and at what level they should begin.

Should every object start as an "atom," the most basic type of class, composing every idea from gravity to elements to buildings and airplanes?

For example, with our cursor lines, should we set a color for each of our points, or should colors be set within our line class? And what if we want to fade between two colors on a single line?

If you build something with classes before you know what you're building, you can easily trap yourself into constructing things that don't make sense, or that can't be adapted to change. Don't get trapped!

In general, you should stick to non-class types when prototyping and exploring your problem. Use lists and numbers to explore your problem, so you can change ideas around easily.

Once you've understood the problem and how to solve it, you can switch to simplifying them into classes. Switching to classes provides the opportunity to simplify things further and to hide away the complicated logic behind it.

Remember, the point of classes is to simplify the things you build and to make it easier to read what you're writing.

Rethinking How We Draw

Now, let's return to our cursors program. Currently, we hold down the space bar to draw our lines. As we do so, we're creating a bunch of +s on the screen.

Of course, it's much easier to draw using the mouse, and to click where we want to make new points. This way, the computer can generate the lines in between the points where we click.

Maybe we should stop thinking in terms of our cursors. Perhaps instead we should start thinking in terms of lines. How do we get from one point to the next?

Well, let's think this through. If we draw a line, we need to know a start point and an end point. By adding more points, we can continue a line, until we reach the last point.

Let's forget about our cursor code for now, and just start drawing again from scratch. We'll see how to create a line, and add points to it, one at a time:

```python
import pygame
import pygame.gfxdraw

pygame.init()

screenWidth = 800
screenHeight = 800

screen = pygame.display.set_mode((screenWidth, screenHeight))

clock = pygame.time.Clock()

white = (255,255,255)
black = (0,0,0)

running = True


plusX = screenWidth // 2
plusY = screenHeight // 2

def draw_flat_line(screen, x1, y1, length, color):
  for x in range(x1, x1 + length):
      pygame.gfxdraw.pixel(screen, x, y1, color)

def draw_vertical_line(screen, x1, y1, length, color):
  for y in range(y1, y1 + length):
      pygame.gfxdraw.pixel(screen, x1, y, color)

def draw_plus_sign(screen, x, y, size, color):
    draw_flat_line(screen, x - (size // 2), y, size, color)
    draw_vertical_line(screen, x, y - (size // 2), size, color)

# Our new array to store points
linePoints = []

while running:
    screen.fill(black)

    draw_plus_sign(screen, plusX, plusY, 15, white)

    # we need at least two points for a line
    if len(linePoints) >= 2:
        # we need to start from the second point in our loop
        for place, point in enumerate(linePoints):
```

```
            if place == 0:
                continue
        pygame.draw.line(screen, white, point, linePoints[place - 1])

    key = pygame.key.get_pressed()

    if key[pygame.K_UP]:
        plusY = plusY - 1
    elif key[pygame.K_DOWN]:
        plusY = plusY + 1

    # add to the list of lines
    if key[pygame.K_SPACE]:
        linePoints.append([plusX, plusY])

    if key[pygame.K_LEFT]:
        plusX = plusX - 1
    elif key[pygame.K_RIGHT]:
        plusX = plusX + 1

    for event in pygame.event.get():
        if event.type == pygame.QUIT: # if you try to quit, let's leave this loop
            running = False
    pygame.display.flip() # this is how we update the screen we've been drawing on.
    clock.tick() # and then we update our clock
```

Drawing with the Mouse

Now let's stop drawing with the keyboard and the arrow keys. They've been nice to begin with and learn, but using our mouse as input will give us better control over the drawing process. (It should also allow us to move more quickly.)

Pygame includes a function for getting the current mouse position. But before we can get the current position, we should make sure the mouse is actually in the Pygame window. To do this, we call another function, `pygame.mouse.get_focused()`, to make sure the mouse is actually in our window. If it is, we set the current x and y position of our cursor to match the mouse using the function `pygame.mouse.get_pos()`, which returns an x and a y position.

To check for our mouse clicks, we'll need a different approach than we used for the keys on the keyboard.

Every mouse click is considered an **event** in Pygame, so we need to check for mouse events in the event portion of our code.

Before we add multiple lines, let's first change our code to use only the mouse. Remember, a lot of minor changes with testing after each is always better than a lot of substantial changes all at once. Fixing broken things is easier if only one thing is changing at a time:

```
import pygame
import pygame.gfxdraw

pygame.init()

screenWidth = 800
screenHeight = 800

screen = pygame.display.set_mode((screenWidth, screenHeight))

clock = pygame.time.Clock()

white = (255,255,255)
black = (0,0,0)

running = True

plusX = screenWidth // 2
plusY = screenHeight // 2

def draw_flat_line(screen, x1, y1, length, color):
  for x in range(x1, x1 + length):
      pygame.gfxdraw.pixel(screen, x, y1, color)

def draw_vertical_line(screen, x1, y1, length, color):
  for y in range(y1, y1 + length):
      pygame.gfxdraw.pixel(screen, x1, y, color)

def draw_plus_sign(screen, x, y, size, color):
```

```
    draw_flat_line(screen, x - (size // 2), y, size, color)
    draw_vertical_line(screen, x, y - (size // 2), size, color)

linePoints = []

while running:
    screen.fill(black)

    # check if the mouse is in the window
    # if it is, set plusX and plusY to the mouse pos
    if pygame.mouse.get_focused():
      plusX, plusY = pygame.mouse.get_pos()

    draw_plus_sign(screen, plusX, plusY, 15, white)

    if len(linePoints) >= 2:
      for place, point in enumerate(linePoints):
        if place == 0:
          continue
        pygame.draw.line(screen, white, point, linePoints[place - 1])

    for event in pygame.event.get():
        # our mouse click gets checked here
        if event.type == pygame.MOUSEBUTTONDOWN:
            if event.button == 1: # left click
               linePoints.append([plusX, plusY])

       if event.type == pygame.QUIT: # if you try to quit, let's leave this loop
            running = False
    pygame.display.flip()
    clock.tick()
```

Running this program yields a new way of drawing our lines, and a different feeling entirely when drawing. We removed the code that allowed us to draw with the arrow key, but we could have left it in.

What do you think would have happened if we did, and you moved the mouse and pressed the keyboard at the same time?

Try it yourself and find out.

Cleaning Up Our Code with Class

Now we have a clean way of adding points to each of our lines. If we wanted, we could also add a function to each of our line objects, so that each would take care of drawing themselves.

Let's do that now, and see what we're capable of with this new way to draw:

```
import pygame
import pygame.gfxdraw

pygame.init()

screenWidth = 800
screenHeight = 800

screen = pygame.display.set_mode((screenWidth, screenHeight))

clock = pygame.time.Clock()

white = (255,255,255)
black = (0,0,0)

running = True

class Line():
    def __init__(self):
        self.linePoints = []

    def __repr__(self):
        if not self.is_line():
            return "Not a line yet."

        return "Line from %s to %s" % (self.linePoints[0], self.linePoints[-1])

    def is_line(self):
        if len(self.linePoints) > 1:
            return True
        return False

    def add_linepoint(self, x, y):
        self.linePoints.append((x, y))
```

```

  def draw_line(self, screen):
    # if we're not a line yet, don't draw!
    if not self.is_line():
      return
    for place, point in enumerate(self.linePoints):
      # skip the first point, there won't be something
      # before it
      if place == 0:
        continue
      pygame.draw.line(screen, white, point, self.linePoints[place - 1])

plusX = screenWidth // 2
plusY = screenHeight // 2

def draw_flat_line(screen, x1, y1, length, color):
 for x in range(x1, x1 + length):
   pygame.gfxdraw.pixel(screen, x, y1, color)

def draw_vertical_line(screen, x1, y1, length, color):
 for y in range(y1, y1 + length):
   pygame.gfxdraw.pixel(screen, x1, y, color)

def draw_plus_sign(screen, x, y, size, color):
  draw_flat_line(screen, x - (size // 2), y, size, color)
  draw_vertical_line(screen, x, y - (size // 2), size, color)

# create our lines of lines with a first new, empty line
lines = [Line()]

while running:
  screen.fill(black)

  if pygame.mouse.get_focused():
   plusX, plusY = pygame.mouse.get_pos()

  draw_plus_sign(screen, plusX, plusY, 15, white)

  for line in lines:
   line.draw_line(screen)

  for event in pygame.event.get():
    # our mouse click gets checked here
    if event.type == pygame.MOUSEBUTTONDOWN:
      if event.button == 1: # left click, add line point
```

```
                lines[-1].add_linepoint(plusX, plusY)

            if event.button == 3: # right click, new line and linepoint
                newLine = Line()
                newLine.add_linepoint(plusX, plusY)
                lines.append(newLine)

        if event.type == pygame.QUIT:
            running = False
    pygame.display.flip()
    clock.tick()
```

All right! We now have a way of making separate lines, and our main loop looks much cleaner. We've been through a lot in this chapter, and our program now might seem a little less cool than it was before this transformation, but we've laid the groundwork for creating new kinds of drawings and new ways of drawing them.

If you find yourself stuck by parts of this chapter, just keep reading. In the next chapter, we'll start seeing why we needed to make our lines into their own class, as we start rewriting the way we draw our lines. When we do this, we'll create totally new ways of drawing lines, and we'll start seeing how we've made creative experimentation even easier.

The preceding code doesn't really do much new. We created a list of Line objects, and then we added points to the last Line in the list (remember that the -1 element is always the last in Python). Then, for right-clicking, we created a new Line object, and started the next line at the right-clicked point.

Mouse Class Lines

Note that if you wanted, you could just as easily make the right-click end the old line, and make the next left-click start the new line.

Now that we have a way of representing lines using our object, let's create new ways of drawing our separate lines.

8

Inventing New Ways to Draw with Shapes

So far, we've only drawn using lines.

In this chapter, we'll change directions and start exploring other ways to draw. We'll try using some of the built-in Pygame shapes, and see if we can find a more interactive, more powerful way to draw in our program.

To begin, let's add a new method to our `Line` object.

We can call it `draw_circle` and make our `for` loop call it instead of the `draw_shape` function:

```
class Line():
    # ... same code from before, add the following lines
    def draw_circle(self, screen):
        for point in self.linePoints:
            pygame.draw.circle(screen, white, point, 5)
```

This new code is easy and is only a minor change. Since we're just drawing each of our points, we don't really need to worry about how many points we use. We just start drawing for each of these points, one at a time.

Does this way of drawing work for you? Are the results pleasant? Try drawing using one of the other built-in Pygame shapes, such as a rectangle or ellipse.

Does that improve things for you? Why not?

Exploring Pygame's Drawing Methods

Pygame provides many more ways of drawing in addition to circles and lines. In fact, if we check what's currently in the library, we can see our options:

```
pygame.draw.rect       #      draw a rectangle shape
pygame.draw.polygon #  draw a shape with any number of sides
pygame.draw.circle     #      draw a circle around a point
pygame.draw.ellipse #  draw a round shape inside a rectangle
pygame.draw.arc  #     draw a partial section of an ellipse
pygame.draw.line       #      draw a straight line segment
```

```
pygame.draw.lines      #     draw multiple contiguous line segments
pygame.draw.aaline     #     draw fine antialiased lines
pygame.draw.aalines #  draw a connected sequence of antialiased lines
```

Remember that all the information about these features is included in the documentation at Pygame.org. If you don't want to open up a web browser and search, you can instead open an IPython shell, and press pygame.draw, followed by the Tab key to see your options.

Experiment with the various drawing functions now, and play around with the shapes. Is there a method that works better for you—a preferred way you'd like to draw with your set of shapes?

Once you've found a new way to draw, let's create a way of switching between drawing methods in our class.

Giving Our Class New Features

We'll need to create a new variable in our class to keep track of how each line should be drawn. Let's call it `drawMode`.

To change drawing modes, we'll add a key check to see whether our user presses one of the numbers on the keypad. One key will mean "draw with lines," and another will mean "draw with circles."

But how do we keep track of the different modes? To do that, we can create global draw mode variables, and set them with unique numbers.

In our case, we'll set them from 1 through 3, so that each new drawing method gets its own number.

Here's what the code might look like:

```
import pygame
import pygame.gfxdraw

import math

```

```
pygame.init()

screenWidth = 800
screenHeight = 800

screen = pygame.display.set_mode((screenWidth, screenHeight))

clock = pygame.time.Clock()

white = (255,255,255)
black = (0,0,0)

running = True

class Line():

    def __init__(self):
        self.linePoints = []
        # Make sure we have a default mode to draw with
        self.draw_mode = 1

    def __repr__(self):
        if not self.is_line():
            return "Not a line yet."

        return "Line from %s to %s" % (self.linePoints[0], self.linePoints[-1])

    def is_line(self):
        if len(self.linePoints) > 1:
            return True
        return False

    def is_shape(self):
        if len(self.linePoints) > 2:
            return True
        return False

    def add_linepoint(self, x, y):
        self.linePoints.append((x, y))

    # New function, to call the right mode of drawing
    def draw(self, screen):
        if self.draw_mode == 1:
            self.draw_line(screen)

```

```
        elif self.draw_mode == 2:
            self.draw_shape(screen)

        elif self.draw_mode == 3:
            self.draw_circle(screen)

    def draw_line(self, screen):
        if not self.is_line():
            return
        for place, point in enumerate(self.linePoints):
            if place == 0:
                continue
            pygame.draw.line(screen, white, point, self.linePoints[place - 1])

    def draw_shape(self, screen):
        if not self.is_line():
            return
        if not self.is_shape():
            self.draw_line(screen)
            return
        pygame.draw.polygon(screen, white, self.linePoints)

    def draw_circle(self, screen):
        for point in self.linePoints:
            pygame.draw.circle(screen, white, point, 5)

plusX = screenWidth // 2
plusY = screenHeight // 2

def draw_flat_line(screen, x1, y1, length, color):
  for x in range(x1, x1 + length):
      pygame.gfxdraw.pixel(screen, x, y1, color)

def draw_vertical_line(screen, x1, y1, length, color):
  for y in range(y1, y1 + length):
      pygame.gfxdraw.pixel(screen, x1, y, color)

def draw_plus_sign(screen, x, y, size, color):
    draw_flat_line(screen, x - (size // 2), y, size, color)
    draw_vertical_line(screen, x, y - (size // 2), size, color)

# create our lines of lines with a first new, empty line
lines = [Line()]

DRAW_LINES = 1
```

```python
DRAW_SHAPE = 2
DRAW_CIRCLES = 3

while running:
    screen.fill(black)

    if pygame.mouse.get_focused():
      plusX, plusY = pygame.mouse.get_pos()

    draw_plus_sign(screen, plusX, plusY, 15, white)

    # Make sure we check which keys are being pressed
    key = pygame.key.get_pressed()

    # Keys 1 - 3 change the shapes for the current line's drawing mode
    if key[pygame.K_1]:
        lines[-1].draw_mode = DRAW_LINES

    if key[pygame.K_2]:
        lines[-1].draw_mode = DRAW_SHAPE

    if key[pygame.K_3]:
        lines[-1].draw_mode = DRAW_CIRCLES


    for line in lines:
      line.draw(screen)

    for event in pygame.event.get():
        # our mouse click gets checked here
        if event.type == pygame.MOUSEBUTTONDOWN:
            if event.button == 1: # left click
                lines[-1].add_linepoint(plusX, plusY)

            if event.button == 3: # right click, new line
                newLine = Line()
                newLine.add_linepoint(plusX, plusY)
                lines.append(newLine)


        if event.type == pygame.QUIT: # if you try to quit, let's leave this loop
            running = False
    pygame.display.flip()
    clock.tick()
```

Now we've added three new drawing modes to our program, and we've also added if statements to ensure that our lines are ready enough for drawing.

If you look at the `draw_shape` function, you'll see that we added first a check for at least two points, and then a check for at least three points.

Because our shape function requires at least 3 points to draw between, we can't send just two points to it without crashing our program.

Making changes like this, and knowing about these kinds of problems before you write code, comes with experience. For now, try getting rid of that double `if` statement, and notice the error message that's generated. This would've been the clue to steer you in the right direction.

We also added checks for the keys being pressed for the numbers 1–3. We added our global variables (in uppercase), so we can tell which drawing method each number represents.

When you run the code, try changing between the different line styles as you draw. If you start combining the different options, you can end up with something interesting like this:

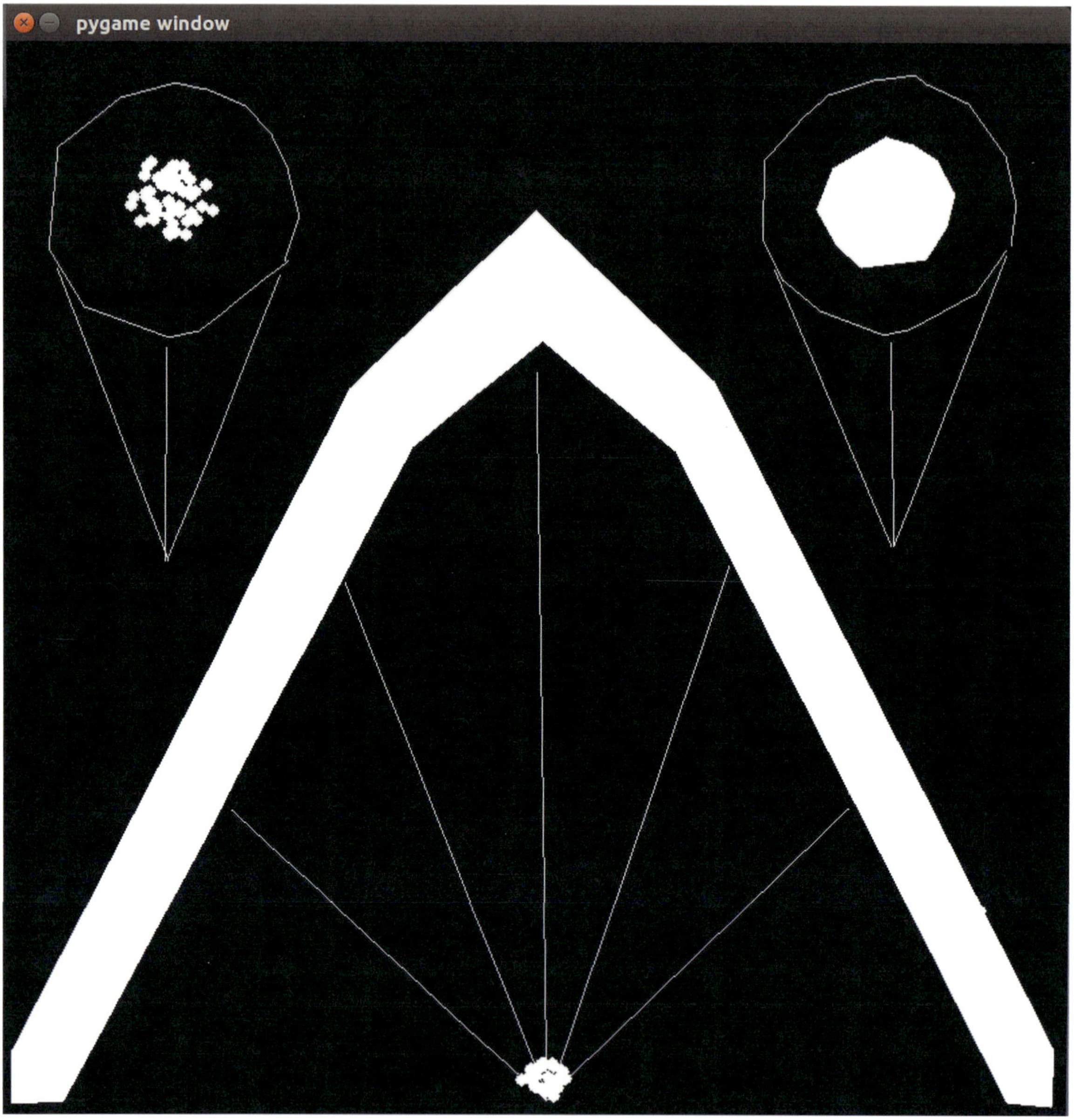

Shapes of New Lines

It's not quite as exciting as our earlier color lines, but it's a start. We can experiment in diverse ways with our ideas as we draw.

Now, let's talk about the code.

First, we added a new default variable for our class, called `draw_mode`. By creating this variable, we eliminate the multiple functions we would have to call to draw in each mode and replace them with a single function, draw.

`Draw()` checks for what `draw_mode` is set to for the current object and then draws using the appropriate function.

Because it might be difficult to remember which of the numbers stands for which drawing method, we created variable names for the numbers 1, 2, and 3 to describe what they are. These variables are all set in capital letters to remind us they shouldn't ever change. Pygame does the same thing, with the keyboard map.

Now each time we draw a line, we can change the drawing style by pressing one of the numbers 1–3 on the keyboard. But as soon as we right-click and start a new line, we've set in stone our line drawing method.

Colorizing Our Lines

Our new drawing method looks great, but it's still missing something. Using only white for all those lines is boring. Let's create a new palette of colors using a list, and pick one of the colors randomly for every line.

To do that, we'll need to pick a set of colors in the RGB palette. A search for "RGB color palette generator" should yield some interesting colors to begin with.

Alternatively, here's a color palette you can use:

```
rainbowPalette =  [(67,121,43), (81, 146, 126), (55, 59, 86), (57, 36, 67),
(83, 57, 92), (126, 28, 61)]
```

With our rainbowPalette defined, we can now use the function random.choice from the random package, and have our lines colored randomly upon creation:

```
# first, make sure you add this line in the top of your program
```

```
import random

# ... and then, in the line class, add to the init function
class Line():

    def __init__(self):
        self.linePoints = []
        self.draw_mode = 1
        self.color = random.choice(rainbowPalette) # make sure we choose a
            random color
    # leave every other function unchange except for the following

    def draw_line(self, screen):
        if not self.is_line():
            return
        for place, point in enumerate(self.linePoints):
            if place == 0:
                continue
            # add the self.color to each line
           pygame.draw.line(screen, self.color, point, self.linePoints[place - 1])

    def draw_shape(self, screen):
        if not self.is_line():
            return
        if not self.is_shape():
            self.draw_line(screen)
            return
        # add the self.color
        pygame.draw.polygon(screen, self.color, self.linePoints)

    def draw_circle(self, screen):
        for point in self.linePoints:
            # add the self.color
            pygame.draw.circle(screen, self.color, point, 5)
```


Here, we've added a `random.choice()`, which takes a random element from our list and sets the line's color to it when the line is created.

We've then updated all our functions to use the self-set color.

And with that, just adding some color makes the drawing experience much better. Now we're really starting to build an interesting creative tool.

Marilyn Mouserow

In the next chapter, we'll add a method of importing images. This will let us bring in images we can trace. We can then save our new starting image and progress and build upon it incrementally.

9

Playing with Files

In this chapter, we'll load images for tracing in our drawing program, add a way of saving our drawings in progress, and finally, create a way to save images from our drawings.

Along the way, we'll learn how to work with the file system, and let our programs write and create new files for us.

Setting Up Our Directories

If you haven't already, it helps to set up a directory for each of your programming projects. I usually do something like this:

```
projectName /
              inputImages/
              outputs/
              main.py
```

With this directories setup, we can keep all the files for our project organized in one spot.

Let's create our directories now. Before we can begin loading images, it would help if we had a place to keep everything separate. Type the following commands into a terminal, or a bash shell (this only works on Linux or MacOS):

```
$ cd ~
$ mkdir Development
$ cd Development
$ mkdir makeartTracer
$ cd makeartTracer
$ mkdir {inputImages,outputs}
$ ls
```

We first change to our home directory. This is always linked to the tilde character (~) and is a shortcut to your user home directory.

Next, we make a directory. We use the command mkdir to make a directory to put our projects in, called "Development".

Next, we change to the Development directory, and then make

our project's new directory, "makeartTracer".

Then, we make two more directories simultaneously by placing braces around the names of the directories we want, separated by a comma.

Finally, we use ls to see whether our new directories were made successfully. (The `ls` command shows us all the subdirectories and files in the current directory. We'd expect to see our newly created subdirectories printed back out.)

If you're following along on Windows, just create a directory called makeartTracer, and then add two subdirectories inside of it, called inputImages and outputs.

Once our directories have been made, it's time to pick an image to use for tracing purposes. I chose a photo of a skateboarder, but you might have your own idea for something you'd like to save. Whatever you choose, save either one image or multiple images to your "inputImages" directory.

Reading Options from the Command Line

We're going to resize the image in our program, so the closer to a square image you've got, the better.

We have a couple options for how we load our images into Python. We could add a file selector window to our program, or we could add an option to the command line. We'll do the latter.

Python has many libraries to take in input from the command line. We'll use one called `argparse`, which lets us save input from the command line as variables in our programs.

Up until now, we've basically had one command for running all our Python programs. It's always been something like this:

```
$ python3 programName.py
```

With `argparse`, we can add more options to running our Python scripts. So, for the above, to add an image named faces.jpg in our "inputImages" directory, we'd do something like this:

```
$ python3 programName.py inputImages/faces.jpg
```

And we'd get that filename passed in to our program. (Note that this isn't the file itself! It's just the filename, `inputImages/faces.jpg`. We'll have to use another library to open the actual file.)

Let's create a new program, called "argTest.py", to start exploring the argparse library:

```
# add the argparse library
import argparse

# create a parser to take in our arguments, describe our program
parser = argparse.ArgumentParser(description='Image tracer')
# add the filename argument to the parser
parser.add_argument('filename')
# create a new object with the parsed arguments
passedIn = parser.parse_args()

print(passedIn)
```

Now, how do we know all these options for the `argparse` library? And how do we know what sorts of things they expect back? Looking at the code above, how would we ever discover that we need to create an `argparser.ArgumentParser`, and then add an argument, and then parse the args? Where does the knowledge of the library like this come from?

There are a few approaches, but the one that works best for me is searching for the example problem. In this case, we might search for "argument parsing python" in Google to find some example code.

Once we've got some example code that looks promising, it's

time to open an IPython shell and test it out. Our IPython shell might look something like this:

```
$ ipython
Python 3.4.3+ (default, Oct 14 2015, 16:03:50)
Type "copyright", "credits" or "license" for more information.

IPython 4.0.3 -- An enhanced Interactive Python.
?          -> Introduction and overview of IPython's features.
%quickref -> Quick reference.
help       -> Python's own help system.
object?    -> Details about 'object', use 'object??' for extra details.

In [1]: %run argTest.py test.img
test.img

In [2]: passedIn
Out[2]: Namespace(filename='test.img')

In [3]: passedIn.filename
Out[3]: 'test.img'
```


In this way, we can start to play around and poke at all the new libraries we're using as we read about them. What do they expect as input, and what do they create as output? Learning to differentiate between the two, and playing around with libraries helps us understand and reason about what's going on, and stops us from playing futile guessing games and changing things back and forth over and over again as we're learning.

Using IPython to Inspect New Libraries

If you get stuck, most libraries are open source, so as a last-ditch effort you can try reading documentation to see how they're built. Some libraries are especially well written, like the requests library in Python.

The %run command from the previous code is especially interesting. It's an IPython-only command that lets us run our script from inside a Python instance, and allows us to see exactly what's happening.

By running the command in the IPython session, we can see interactively what each object is from the program we ran. Just type in the object's name, and hit Enter. We can print each object.

To see what's available in one of our imported libraries, we can just type the name of the imported library, and then type "." and press the Tab key. We'll automatically get a list of all the options within that library.

But back to the point. We now have a method of adding and importing filenames into our program when we run it. Let's add a way to show the image as a background, as well as a way to hide and display it.

I'll use the **b** and **v** keys on the keyboard to hide and show the image I'm tracing.

```
import pygame
import pygame.gfxdraw

import random

from pygame.locals import *

import math

import argparse

parser = argparse.ArgumentParser(description='Image tracer')
parser.add_argument('filename')
passedIn = parser.parse_args()

imageFile = pygame.image.load(passedIn.filename)
imageFile = pygame.transform.scale(imageFile, (800,800))

pygame.init()
```

```python

screenWidth = 800
screenHeight = 800

screen = pygame.display.set_mode((screenWidth, screenHeight))

clock = pygame.time.Clock()

white = (255,255,255)
black = (0,0,0)
rainbowPalette =  [(67,121,43), (81, 146, 126), (55, 59, 86), (57, 36, 67), (83, 57, 92),
(126, 28, 61), (148, 47, 37), (173, 50, 6), (188, 84, 29), (164, 118, 41), (197, 190, 20)]

running = True
backgroundVisible = True

class Line():

    def __init__(self):
        self.linePoints = []
        # Make sure we have a default mode to draw with
        self.draw_mode = 1
        self.color = random.choice(rainbowPalette)

    def __repr__(self):
        if not self.is_line():
            return "Not a line yet."

        return "Line from %s to %s" % (self.linePoints[0], self.linePoints[-1])

    def is_line(self):
        if len(self.linePoints) > 1:
            return True
        return False

    def is_shape(self):
        if len(self.linePoints) > 2:
            return True
        return False

    def add_linepoint(self, x, y):
        self.linePoints.append((x, y))

    # New function, to call the right mode of drawing
    def draw(self, screen):
```

```
    if self.draw_mode == 1:
      self.draw_line(screen)

    elif self.draw_mode == 2:
      self.draw_shape(screen)

    elif self.draw_mode == 3:
      self.draw_circle(screen)

  def draw_line(self, screen):
    if not self.is_line():
      return
    for place, point in enumerate(self.linePoints):
      if place == 0:
        continue
      pygame.draw.line(screen, self.color, point, self.linePoints[place - 1])

  def draw_shape(self, screen):
    if not self.is_line():
      return
    if not self.is_shape():
      self.draw_line(screen)
      return
    pygame.draw.polygon(screen, self.color, self.linePoints)

  def draw_circle(self, screen):
    for point in self.linePoints:
      pygame.draw.circle(screen, self.color, point, 5)

plusX = screenWidth // 2
plusY = screenHeight // 2

def draw_flat_line(screen, x1, y1, length, color):
 for x in range(x1, x1 + length):
   pygame.gfxdraw.pixel(screen, x, y1, color)

def draw_vertical_line(screen, x1, y1, length, color):
 for y in range(y1, y1 + length):
   pygame.gfxdraw.pixel(screen, x1, y, color)

def draw_plus_sign(screen, x, y, size, color):
  draw_flat_line(screen, x - (size // 2), y, size, color)
  draw_vertical_line(screen, x, y - (size // 2), size, color)

# create our lines of lines with a first new, empty line
```

```python
lines = [Line()]

DRAW_LINES = 1
DRAW_SHAPE = 2
DRAW_CIRCLES = 3

while running:
    if backgroundVisible:
        screen.blit(imageFile, (0,0))
    else:
        screen.fill(black)

    if pygame.mouse.get_focused():
      plusX, plusY = pygame.mouse.get_pos()

    draw_plus_sign(screen, plusX, plusY, 15, white)

    # Make sure we check which keys are being pressed
    key = pygame.key.get_pressed()

    if key[pygame.K_v]:
        backgroundVisible = True
    if key[pygame.K_b]:
        backgroundVisible = False

    # Keys 1 - 3 change the shapes for the current line's drawing mode
    if key[pygame.K_1]:
        lines[-1].draw_mode = DRAW_LINES

    if key[pygame.K_2]:
        lines[-1].draw_mode = DRAW_SHAPE

    if key[pygame.K_3]:
        lines[-1].draw_mode = DRAW_CIRCLES


    for line in lines:
      line.draw(screen)

    for event in pygame.event.get():
        # our mouse click gets checked here
        if event.type == pygame.MOUSEBUTTONDOWN:
            if event.button == 1: # left click
                lines[-1].add_linepoint(plusX, plusY)

```

```
            if event.button == 3: # right click, new line
                newLine = Line()
                newLine.add_linepoint(plusX, plusY)
                lines.append(newLine)


        if event.type == pygame.QUIT:
            running = False
    pygame.display.flip()
    clock.tick()
```

There are a few things to note with our new code.

We've put the drawing of the image at the beginning of our loop, so our line drawing function writes over the existing image. If we'd put our line drawing loop before we drew the image, we wouldn't be able to see anything, because the `screen.blit` would write over what we'd drawn already.

We also added a new variable called `backgroundVisible`. It's set as a Boolean value, meaning it can only be True or False. We set it to True by default, but when we want to see just the drawing we set it to False.

This is what I ended up with after tracing around a new image:

Traced Skateboarder

After drawing with the program for a while, I noticed a few things that could be improved.

First, I don't have an Undo, and I don't have a way to save the lines I've drawn. I really want to save my drawings with all their lines.

Saving Our Drawings with Pickle

Luckily, Python includes the **pickle** library for loading and saving any Python object. We'll make it so pressing the letter s saves our lines into a pickle file. We'll then be able to point to this saved pickle file to reload our drawing. Let's try it now:

```
import pygame
import pygame.gfxdraw

import random

from pygame.locals import *

import math

import argparse
import pickle

parser = argparse.ArgumentParser(description='Image tracer')
parser.add_argument('filename')
# add the drawing as an optional argument
parser.add_argument('-d', '--drawing', help='Filename of a drawing to load')
passedIn = parser.parse_args()


imageFile = pygame.image.load(passedIn.filename)
imageFile = pygame.transform.scale(imageFile, (800,800))

pygame.init()

screenWidth = 800
screenHeight = 800

screen = pygame.display.set_mode((screenWidth, screenHeight))

clock = pygame.time.Clock()

white = (255,255,255)
black = (0,0,0)
rainbowPalette = [(67,121,43), (81, 146, 126), (55, 59, 86), (57, 36, 67), (83, 57, 92),
(126, 28, 61), (148, 47, 37), (173, 50, 6), (188, 84, 29), (164, 118, 41), (197, 190, 20)]

```

```python
running = True
backgroundVisible = True


class Line():

    def __init__(self):
        self.linePoints = []
        # Make sure we have a default mode to draw with
        self.draw_mode = 1
        self.color = random.choice(rainbowPalette)

    def __repr__(self):
        if not self.is_line():
            return "Not a line yet."

        return "Line from %s to %s" % (self.linePoints[0], self.linePoints[-1])

    def is_line(self):
        if len(self.linePoints) > 1:
            return True
        return False

    def is_shape(self):
        if len(self.linePoints) > 2:
            return True
        return False

    def add_linepoint(self, x, y):
        self.linePoints.append((x, y))

    # New function, to call the right mode of drawing
    def draw(self, screen):
        if self.draw_mode == 1:
            self.draw_line(screen)

        elif self.draw_mode == 2:
            self.draw_shape(screen)

        elif self.draw_mode == 3:
            self.draw_circle(screen)

    def draw_line(self, screen):
        if not self.is_line():
            return
```

```
        for place, point in enumerate(self.linePoints):
            if place == 0:
                continue
           pygame.draw.line(screen, self.color, point, self.linePoints[place - 1])

    def draw_shape(self, screen):
        if not self.is_line():
            return
        if not self.is_shape():
            self.draw_line(screen)
            return
        pygame.draw.polygon(screen, self.color, self.linePoints)

    def draw_circle(self, screen):
        for point in self.linePoints:
            pygame.draw.circle(screen, self.color, point, 5)

plusX = screenWidth // 2
plusY = screenHeight // 2

def draw_flat_line(screen, x1, y1, length, color):
  for x in range(x1, x1 + length):
      pygame.gfxdraw.pixel(screen, x, y1, color)

def draw_vertical_line(screen, x1, y1, length, color):
  for y in range(y1, y1 + length):
      pygame.gfxdraw.pixel(screen, x1, y, color)

def draw_plus_sign(screen, x, y, size, color):
    draw_flat_line(screen, x - (size // 2), y, size, color)
    draw_vertical_line(screen, x, y - (size // 2), size, color)

# If we've got a drawing, load it, otherwise, new empty line
if passedIn.drawing:
    lines = pickle.load(open(passedIn.drawing, 'rb'))
else:
    lines = [Line()]

DRAW_LINES = 1
DRAW_SHAPE = 2
DRAW_CIRCLES = 3

while running:
    if backgroundVisible:
        screen.blit(imageFile, (0,0))
```

```python
    else:
        screen.fill(black)

    if pygame.mouse.get_focused():
      plusX, plusY = pygame.mouse.get_pos()

    draw_plus_sign(screen, plusX, plusY, 15, white)

    # Make sure we check which keys are being pressed
    key = pygame.key.get_pressed()

    if key[pygame.K_v]:
        backgroundVisible = True
    if key[pygame.K_b]:
        backgroundVisible = False

    # Keys 1 - 3 change the shapes for the current line's drawing mode
    if key[pygame.K_1]:
        lines[-1].draw_mode = DRAW_LINES

    if key[pygame.K_2]:
        lines[-1].draw_mode = DRAW_SHAPE

    if key[pygame.K_3]:
        lines[-1].draw_mode = DRAW_CIRCLES

    # add the 's' key to save a file called 'lines.pkl'
    if key[pygame.K_s]:
        pickle.dump(lines, open('lines.pkl', 'wb'))

    for line in lines:
      line.draw(screen)

    for event in pygame.event.get():
        # our mouse click gets checked here
        if event.type == pygame.MOUSEBUTTONDOWN:
            if event.button == 1: # left click
                lines[-1].add_linepoint(plusX, plusY)

            if event.button == 3: # right click, new line
                newLine = Line()
                newLine.add_linepoint(plusX, plusY)
                lines.append(newLine)
```

```
        if event.type == pygame.QUIT: # if you try to quit, let's leave this loop
            running = False
    pygame.display.flip()
    clock.tick()
```

To run this program, we now have a few options we can pass it. We can start with our image to trace, trace a line or two, and then save it out. We can then close the program, and pass in the Pickle file to continue where we left off.

Let's try that now. Start with the new image, and try tracing around it with a drawing you have. When you're done, hit s to save the image.

Once you've drawn something you like, save it, and close the program. You can launch the program again and see your saved work by calling it from the command line with the file you've saved:

```
$ python3 traceImageLoader.py sourceImages/barrel.jpeg -d lines.pkl
```

Now when you run your program, you should see the drawings you've made from before.

If we step through the changes we've made in the code, we'll see that we've only done two new things. We incorporated a way of telling Python which pickle file to load, and we created a way to save a single pickle file. To save multiple drawings, we must rename the file after it's been saved; otherwise, it will be overwritten the next time we hit `s` in the app.

Adding Undo to Our Program

After drawing for a while, do you notice any improvements you'd like to make to the app? An Undo, perhaps?

Writing an Undo feature should be easy enough to do, especially if you only do one level of Undo, and no Redo. You'd only have to make sure that you have more than one point on your current line, and then delete the last point. Maybe you could even go all the way back to the beginning of the line. But after that, how would you manage an Undo through each of the lines you've drawn?

You could keep track of the length of all the lines, and as we went back down to nothing left, we could delete the current line and keep going back, all the way down to the very first line we drew.

Let's create a new key to step back and undo things. Let's use the `z` key, and see how well that works. Remember, our keyboard might be sending many commands at once, so we might not get the behavior we expect at first, and our Undo might accidentally perform a bunch of undo's. We'll insert a new `if` statement right in our event loop, and then do our logic on undos right there.

```
while running:
    # the rest of our code is fine, just add this to the loop
    if key[pygame.K_z]:
        # if the last point on the current line
        if len(lines[-1].linePoints) == 1:
            # if there's more than one line remaining,
            # delete the current line
            if len(lines) > 1:
                del lines[-1] # remove the last line
        # if we have more than one line point
        elif len(lines[-1].linePoints) > 1:
            # delete the last linepoint
            del lines[-1].linePoints[-1]
```

This code is rather difficult to read and think about. We have a lot of `if` statements that are hard to read, and it's extremely difficult to think about what's going on. Even worse, when we press the `z` button on the keyboard with our current code, it doesn't just go back one step, it goes back many steps.

Let's deal with the ugliness of this code and get it working properly. Currently, we're going back a bunch of steps at a time, because we're not checking to see whether we've pressed the button recently.

Using Time to Add Delay to Our Undo

Let's add yet another library, "time," to our program.

Before adding the `time` library, however, let's open up another IPython shell and see if we can understand how it works:

```
$ ipython
Python 3.4.3+ (default, Oct 14 2015, 16:03:50)
Type "copyright", "credits" or "license" for more information.

IPython 4.0.3 -- An enhanced Interactive Python.
?         -> Introduction and overview of IPython's features.
%quickref -> Quick reference.
help      -> Python's own help system.
object?   -> Details about 'object', use 'object??' for extra details.
In [1]: import time
In [2]: time.time()
Out[2]: 1465957887.8971229

In [3]: time.time()
Out[3]: 1465957890.2141368
```

Woah. What could that mean? By doing `time.time` a few times in a row, I can see that it seems to represent seconds. So, each of those numbers represents a second, and the decimal represents the parts of the seconds.

But how many seconds is that from? When did that count begin? For Unix and Python, the zeroth second, the one from which we start counting, is January 1st, 1970. If we're on another platform, we can see where we start counting from with the function `time.gmtime(0)`. Neat.

But back to the time we're working with. We need a way to measure how much time has passed since the last button was pressed. Let's create a new variable outside of our loop, called `lastPressed`, and set it to when the program starts.

Now, we can add another check to our `if` statement from before, and see whether enough time has passed to allow another Undo to happen:

```
# right now we're undoing ever 200 miliseconds
if key[pygame.K_z] and time.time() > (lastPressed + .2):
    lastPressed = time.time()
    # if the last point on the line
    if len(lines[-1].linePoints) == 1:
        if len(lines) > 1:
            del lines[-1] # remove the last line
    elif len(lines[-1].linePoints) > 1:
        del lines[-1].linePoints[-1]
```


Try playing with the delay value to get the right amount that works for you. Now when we run the program, we can see our Undo path occur more slowly.

Now that we have our Undo occurring at a more reasonable rate, how could we make the preceding code more legible? Remember, must always get our code working properly first, and then we can go back and make it look right for the people who will read it after us. Let's do that now.

Protecting Ourselves from Errors

What are we really checking here? Are we checking for the length of each of the lines? We're already checking for the length of the array of lines, so we could probably leave it at that. But for each of the line objects? We could probably improve our code's readability by creating a new function in the Line class that returns the length of the linePoints array.

Let's add a new function in the `Line` class called `num_points`. We'll have it return the length of the `linePoints` list. Then, replace the preceding code with something more legible:

```
if key[pygame.K_z] and time.time() > (lastPressed + .2):
    lastPressed = time.time()
    # if the last point on the line
    if lines[-1].num_points() == 1:
        if len(lines) > 1:
            del lines[-1] # remove the last line
    elif lines[-1].num_points() > 1:
        del lines[-1].linePoints[-1]
```

This is close enough for now. It's still an ugly piece of code, but it's mostly legible.

Now that we've got Undo working with our code, and we can change our drawing mode types, we finally have a way of drawing something that's half decent. Plus, with the ability to save our drawings, we can start work that spans multiple drawing sessions.

What would you want to build next? Now that we've got a solid foundation for drawing using points, let's take a step back and look at images. In the next chapter, we'll learn how to make our drawings come to life by turning them into gifs. We'll also start breaking them in innovative ways with some basic glitching.

Painting with Images

Well, not quite a painting...

In this chapter, we'll take a side trip, and learn to manipulate images in our programs. We'll walk through how images work, and how they're loaded and saved. Finally, we'll learn to transform a series of images into movies.

Along the way, we'll also learn how to break images, creating new, glitched versions of the things we've made. Hopefully we'll also learn something new about the way our computers work.

As we go along, you can either use your own images or the ones we'll use in this chapter. The images can be downloaded at the makeartwithpython.com site.

If you remember from the first chapter, images are just lists of pixels, grouped together. They'll be thousands or millions of tuples, each with a red, green, and blue value. (Remember, tuples are like lists you can't change, and they're surrounded by parentheses, just like lists.)

Well, that's not entirely true. Depending on the image type, they might not even have a red, green, and blue (RGB) value. Instead they might have a cyan, yellow, magenta, and black (CMYK) color. Or, they might just have a black and a white value. Or even a red, green, blue, and transparency value.

As we saw previously when we chose our colors, these values can go from 0–255 in Pygame. But the same isn't true everywhere. Another library other than Pygame might have values from 0–1, with each value being a decimal. It's important to check with each library you use to determine how they calculate the range of values for colors, as well as what colors they assume exist.

Dissecting an Image

Let's start by jumping into an IPython shell and opening an image to see for ourselves. We'll use the "Pillow" library and see just how Pillow lets us view and manipulate images.

```
$ pip3 install pillow
$ IPython
Python 3.4.3 (default, May 1 2015, 19:14:18)
Type "copyright", "credits" or "license" for more infor\
mation.

IPython 4.1.2 -- An enhanced Interactive Python.
?         -> Introduction and overview of IPython's features.
%quickref -> Quick reference.
help      -> Python's own help system.
object?   -> Details about 'object', use 'object??' for extra details.

In [1]: from PIL import Image

In [2]: a = Image.open('images/skater.jpeg') # replace with your image path

In [3]: a
Out[3]: <PIL.JpegImagePlugin.JpegImageFile image mode=RGB size=5760x3840 at
   0x110A842E8>

In [4]: a.size
Out[4]: (5760, 3840)

In [5]: b = a.load()

In [6]: b[0,0]
Out[6]: (13, 9, 10)

In [7]: b[0,0] = (255, 255, 255)

In [8]: a.show()
```

The Skater.jpeg file

First, we install the Pillow library using pip. We use pip to install almost all Python libraries.

Next, we open an IPython shell to experiment with the way Pillow loads images.

Looking at the preceding code, you might have noticed that we don't use a two-dimensional array like normal. Instead, we send the two coordinates for which we'd like to see values, inside of one of the array's brackets.

Instead of what we'd expect, `[0][0]`, we access the first pixel's RGB values like this: `[0,0]`.

Pillow works like this to make things faster. When working with individual pixels on larger images, it can take a lot of memory to maintain the lists as standard Python lists. Instead, we access it in this way, so things can be looked up more quickly. It's not really something you need to know the details about, but it is one of those tricky parts that can trip you up if you're not aware.

When we open an image, we don't immediately have access to all its pixels. This is because Pillow is used mostly for resizing images, so it doesn't load the image for processing until we call `.load()`. This tells Python to load all the image pixels into memory, so each can be edited individually.

When we address the pixel at `[0,0]`, we can see what's waiting there for us. In this case, for the `brooklyn.jpg` image, it's the RGB color `(13, 9, 10)`. Again, this is returned as a tuple, because it's a smaller footprint in memory. If you're using your own image, you may have different values.

Finally, let's set the first pixel to be white. This way, we can confirm that we are able to edit the image. We then call `a.show()`, a function to display the modified image in a new window.

Great! Now how do we do something interesting?

Manipulating Whole Images

Let's see. We could just save out the new image we just made, but that would be boring. We could also import other images and paste them over our existing image. Maybe that would be a bit better? Let's see if we can continue with our existing code, but this time we'll also try rotating our image.

```
from PIL import Image

im = Image.open("images/skater.jpeg")
im.rotate(45).show()
im.show()
```

Source Image Rotated and Flipped with Pillow

In the preceding code, keep in mind that we're stringing together two different function calls in the same line. When we do this, we make it so that after every function, the result gets sent to the next function. So, at the end of this call, we show the image, but the original image isn't changed at all, because the rotated image isn't assigned to anything.

You can see this with the next window that opens. If you don't run this in an IPython shell, and you run it in a Python script, you'll see one image and then the other.

Now what else can we do with this flipping function?

Making Mirror Images

Let's try creating something fun by copying and pasting and re-scaling an image repeatedly.

We'll start by resizing the image to 512 x 512 and then repeating and flipping it over itself, like a mirror image:

```python
import PIL
from PIL import Image, ImageOps

# Let's set up our command line arguments
import argparse
parser = argparse.ArgumentParser(description="Image flipper")
parser.add_argument('-i', '--image', help='Filename of input image', required=True)
parser.add_argument('-o', '--output', help="Output file", default='output.jpg', required=True)
passedIn = parser.parse_args()

# Output image size
finalSize = 1024, 1024

# Input image resize
size = 512, 512

# Open our passed in image filename
im = Image.open(str(passedIn.image))

# Resize it to the size above, using a resize algorithm called LANCZOS
im = im.resize(size, PIL.Image.LANCZOS)

# Create a new blank RGB image
out = Image.new('RGB', finalSize)

# Paste in the first rescaled image at top left corner (0,0)
out.paste(im, (0,0))

# Paste second image mirror in center
out.paste(ImageOps.mirror(im), (512,0))

# Paste upside down image below first image
# Flip function mirrors vertically
out.paste(ImageOps.flip(im), (0, 512))

# Paste last mirror image below second image
# Flipped horizontally and vertically
out.paste(ImageOps.flip(ImageOps.mirror(im)), (512,512))

# Save the image out
out.save(passedIn.output)
```

Now, to run the above code we just got back to the command line, and give it an input image filename. It's probably best if your image is already square, because if it isn't, it'll be squished to become a square:

```
$ python3 imageFlipper.py -h
usage: imageFlipper.py [-h] [-i IMAGE] [-o OUTPUT]

Image flipper

optional arguments:
  -h, --help            show this help message and exit
  -i IMAGE, --image IMAGE
                        Filename of input image
  -o OUTPUT, --output OUTPUT
                        Output file

$ python3 imageFlipper.py -i brooklyn.jpeg -o output.png
```

After running the preceding code, you should now see a new image named "output.png". Open it and take a look. Did it have a favorable effect on your original image? Here's my image:

Source Image Rotated with Pillow

Now let's get wild and try something totally different. Let's make a spiral of the same image, flipped in on itself. We'll perform this process repeatedly, ending up with something completely new and different.

I saw an image like the one show below and decided I wanted to try to achieve the same effect with the image we were just using:

Another Image Painting

We can tell that we're rotating and shrinking the same square, over and over again. We draw a square, rotate it a bit, shrink it from where it was, and continue.

Rather than trying to perfect this, however, let's start experimenting with something we could do similarly.

Creating Geometric Images

We could, for example, try making an image that is copied onto itself, rotated, and made smaller.

In this case, it could really help to draw out what we want to do with paper and pencil, and to think through all the pieces we'll need to do it.

Let's start by thinking about the image that we'll transform. We'd like to rotate it around a center point. That should probably be the center of the entire initial image.

So, how do we do that?

If we look at the Pygame documentation, we find that there is a whole part of the library called `transform`. This is where we'll find all the things we need to do.

Again, if we look at our source image, we can see what's happening is that the image is being made smaller, it's being rotated, and it's being copied and pasted into itself.

We must also be sure that if we're pasting an image that will be rotated, we first transform our surface to RGBA, so we don't have colored space surrounding our pasted image.

Let's see how to create a transparent surface, and make sure it's RGBA:

```
# First, let's load and then copy our input image
newImage = pygame.image.load(passedIn.image)
blankImage = newImage.copy()

# Next, let's make sure they're both 'RGBA', so parts can be invisible
newImage = newImage.convert_alpha()
blankImage = blankImage.convert_alpha()

# Finally, let's make sure we know how big our image is
imageWidth = newImage.get_width()
imageHeight = newImage.get_height()
```

At this point in our code, **`blankImage`** isn't really blank. It's just a copy of what the input image was from the command line, which is fine in this instance. We'll change its size soon, which will let us paste without edges showing.

Now, let's think though what we want to have happen to our images. We want them to get progressively smaller, and we want them to get progressively less rotated, so let's try that out, using the square root function:


```
# Scale image to fit
scaler = 10
rotate = passedIn.rotate
for i in range(60):
    scaled = pygame.transform.scale(newImage, [int(imageWidth - sqrt(scaler)),
      int(imageHeight - sqrt(imageHeight))])

    rotatedScaled = pygame.transform.rotate(scaled, sqrt(rotate))
    rotatedCorner = rotatePoint(scaler, scaler, imageWidth // 2, imageHeight
      // 2, sqrt(rotate))
    blankImage.blit(rotatedScaled, rotatedCorner)
    scaler += 10
    rotate += rotate

pygame.image.save(blankImage, passedIn.output)
```

There's a lot happening here. First, we create a new variable to keep track of how much we scale our image, and then we create another to keep track of how much we rotate our image.

After this, we have a loop for 60 occurrences of shrinking and copying the image in on itself.

The first line in this loop creates and assigns a new image to the scaled version of the image. We send in the original image every time because of the way Pygame scales rotated images. If we didn't do this, our image would change in total size as it rotated, and that's not what we want.

Next, we rotate by the square root of our current rotation, and then we create a rotated point that matches our rotation from before, again rotating around the center of our image.

Finally, we copy this transformed image back into the `blankImage`, at the position we just calculated with the call to the `rotatePoint` function. By the way, the function for rotating around a point is below:

```
def rotatePoint(x1, y1, x2, y2, rotate):
    '''
    Rotates around x1, y2 by rotate degrees
    '''
    inRadians = radians(rotate)
    nx = cos(inRadians) * (x1 - x2) - sin(inRadians) * (y1 - y2) + x2
    ny = sin(inRadians) * (x1 - x2) + cos(inRadians) * (y1 - y2) + y2

    return int(nx), int(ny)
```

You'll see that our function runs on degrees rather than radians as in Pygame. So, we'll need to make sure we keep track of the right things, and make sure the number we pass in gets translated properly.

In case you've forgotten, we translate degrees into radians like so:

```
inRadians = pi * degrees / 180 # pi is available in math.pi
```

Because we're now using `math.pi`, we'll need to import it into our program. We can either import it with `import math`, and then math.pi when we need it, or from math import pi, and then just refer to it as pi anywhere we need it in our program.

With the last two pieces of code, we can finally make our program run, and do something. Let's try that now, putting it all together:

```
scaler = 10
rotate = float(passedIn.rotate)
for i in range(30):
    scaled = pygame.transform.scale(newImage, [int(imageWidth - sqrt(scaler)),
      int(imageHeight - sqrt(imageHeight))])

    blankImage.blit(pygame.transform.rotate(scaled, sqrt(pi * rotate / 180)),
rotatePoint(scaler, scaler, imageWidth // 2, imageHeight // 2, sqrt(rotate)))
    scaler += 10
    rotate += rotate

pygame.image.save(blankImage, passedIn.output)
```

With this, we finally have our image. We can see whether or not we get something that looks good.

In my case, I'm not sure whether I like the image. It seems too cramped in that little window. What can I do about this?

Let's try making a mirror image of the copied image we've made. We'll double the size of the width and height of the image, and try mirroring and flipping the image in on itself.

```
# after the pygame.image.save from above

# create a new surface, twice as big in each dimension
doubleOut = pygame.Surface((imageWidth * 2, imageHeight * 2))
# copy the above image to the top left corner
doubleOut.blit(blankImage, (0,0))
# copy a flipped image to the center top corner
doubleOut.blit(pygame.transform.flip(blankImage, True, False), (imageWidth, 0))
# copy a flipped rotated image to the bottom left corner
doubleOut.blit(pygame.transform.flip(pygame.transform.rotate(blankImage, 180),
      True, False), (0, imageHeight))
# copy a rotated image to the bottom middle corner
doubleOut.blit(pygame.transform.rotate(blankImage, 180), (imageWidth, imageHeight))
```

```
# save it with the word 'mirror_' in front of the file name passed in
pygame.image.save(doubleOut, 'mirror_' + passedIn.output)
```

The preceding code includes comments that explain what's happening, but just so we know…

Each of our `pygame.transform` calls returns an image and doesn't change the image that is sent. So, we have function calls in place for each of the transforms we perform, and if we need more than one transformation, we can have each transformation sent directly to the next.

Look at the image that you get. Does it look interesting? Try changing the number of degrees you start with. Do things get better, or worse?

In my case, the image now almost looks passable—almost looks interesting.

Turning Our Images into Videos

Now let's take things even further by transforming our program into a video, by writing a new program that will run this program. Sound crazy? Let's try it!

The first thing we need to do is edit our original program. It was saving out each version of our image with the prefix "mirror_". Let's change that so it just saves out our mirror image as the main image:

```
# comment out the first save
# pygame.image.save(blankImage, passedIn.output)
doubleOut = pygame.Surface((imageWidth * 2, imageHeight * 2))
doubleOut.blit(blankImage, (0,0))
doubleOut.blit(pygame.transform.flip(blankImage, True, False), (imageWidth, 0))
doubleOut.blit(pygame.transform.flip(pygame.transform.rotate(blankImage, 180),
      True, False), (0, imageHeight))
doubleOut.blit(pygame.transform.rotate(blankImage, 180), (imageWidth, imageHeight))
```

```
# and get rid of the mirror_ prefix
pygame.image.save(doubleOut, passedIn.output)
```

Next, let's write a program that repeatedly calls the program we've already written. We'll use two new Python libraries, `subprocess` and `os`. From `subprocess` we'll use the `call` function, which lets us send a list of strings to make the command line run.

From `os`, we'll use the function to check whether a directory exists. If it doesn't, we'll call the command for making a directory in Linux.

```
import argparse
parser = argparse.ArgumentParser(description="Image flipper animator")
parser.add_argument('-i', '--image', help='Filename of input image')
passedIn = parser.parse_args()

from subprocess import call
import os

# if there isn't a directory called output, make it
# all the images will go there
if not os.path.isdir('output/'):
    call(['mkdir', 'output'])

# for now let's start at 0 and go through a perfect loop
for i in range(360):
    print('Doing number %i', i)
    call(['python3', 'imageFractalPygame.py', '-i', passedIn.image, '-o', 'output/'
          + str(i) + '.jpg', '-r', str(i)])

# after we're done, turn it into a movie using this command
# ffmpeg -i %d.jpg -profile:v high -level 4.0 -strict -2 out.mp4

call(['ffmpeg', '-i', 'output/%d.jpg', '-profile:v', 'high', '-level',
    '4.0', '-strict', '-2', 'out.mp4'])
```

In this new program, we just take in one input, the source image, to run through and process from 0 to 359 degrees. We go all the way to 359 so that we get a perfect loop at the end of our video.

Here again, we added the call function, and we can see that our new program call gets run every time. If we wanted, we could use a Python function built in to all strings called `split()` to break up the original command into a list of strings. It works by reading a string for a match of whatever you pass to it, and then splitting the string at each point in the match. We'll use a space to match every space in the string:

```
In [2]: makeDirectory = 'mkdir output'.split(' ')

In [3]: makeDirectory
Out[3]: ['mkdir', 'output']
```

See if you can make your program more readable by taking advantage of this feature for both of the subprocesses we call. Now, if you have `ffmpeg` installed, you should see two new things after letting this program run for a while. First, you'll notice that you won't really be able to use your computer at all while the program is running, because Pygame keeps opening up and taking control of your screen.

(If you don't have `ffmpeg` installed, just remember that on Ubuntu Linux it's as easy as doing a `sudo apt-get install ffmpeg` in your terminal. For every other operating system, you'll need to follow their specific installation instructions from the ffmpeg site.)

Second, you should see that you've got a new directory, called "output" that contains all 360 of your images, in a perfect circle. Going through each of these images, you should be able to get a feel for how your program works, and see what changing the number of degrees does for it.

Finally, if you open the video we made, you should see the process we built, and the image rotating in on itself. There's a lot happening here, and maybe the image itself seems too chaotic for a video. If that's the case, just take a few frames you like and make them into a gif instead.

We finally have a way of creating and distorting our own images. In the next chapter, we'll try drawing with the images we have, incorporating them back into the lines we've built so far, to see if we can make something new and interesting with our new knowledge.

11
Drawing Infinities

Let's talk about the plane. No, I don't mean the aircraft; I mean the imaginary two-dimensional surface that stretches on forever, like tiles in our houses, where the same pattern repeats itself forever.

Lately, I've been daydreaming about making tiled images like the kind M.C. Escher used to make. But drawing such images is difficult, and I'd rather use a computer to explore how his drawings work.

M.C. Escher created artistic tessellations, which is the term mathematicians use for when a two-dimensional plane is tiled infinitely without any gaps.

The Three Regular Polygons that Tesselate the Plane

Regardless of all that, what's the simplest thing we can draw to tile the plane?

A few simple shapes that tile the plane include the square, the triangle, and the hexagon.

As it turns out, you can create the hexagon using the triangles. So, if we're just using the "basic" polygons, we can choose the triangle or the square.

My computer monitor is already a square, which is rather boring, so let's start instead with the triangle.

Pygame doesn't have a built-in way of telling it to draw a triangle with equal sides. Instead, it just has a function for drawing polygons. We'll need to figure out how to draw equal-sided polygons.

Drawing A Centered Triangle

So, how do we figure out how to draw an equal-sided polygon? Performing a search on StackOverflow.com (the programmers' help community) provides an answer. We should start with a center point, move straight up to get the first corner, and get the other two corners in increments of 120 degrees on a circle around the center point.

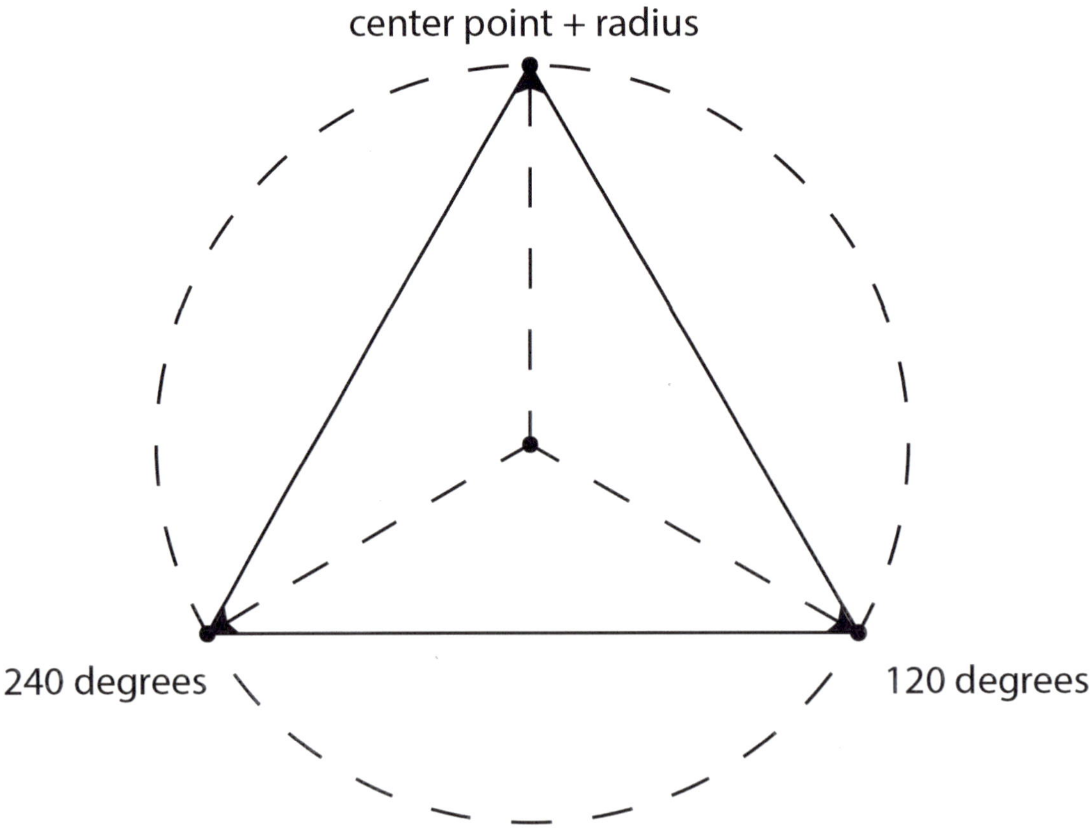

Drawing a triangle from a center point

Let's write out the function for rotating points around a center point, and check that it works by sending it our two points.

Our centered triangle function looks like this:

```
from math import cos, sin

def create_centered_triangle(center, radius):
    # the top of the triangle
    C1 = [center[0], center[1] - radius]

    # the bottom right
    r120 = {'cos': cos(radians(120)), 'sin': sin(radians(120))}
    # the bottom left
    r240 = {'cos': cos(radians(240)), 'sin': sin(radians(240))}

    rX = [C1[0] - center[0] , C1[1] - center[1]]
    rL, rR = [0, 0], [0, 0]

    rL[0] = rX[0] * r120['cos'] - rX[1] * r120['sin']
    rL[1] = rX[0] * r120['sin'] + rX[1] * r120['cos']
    rR[0] = rX[0] * r240['cos'] - rX[1] * r240['sin']
    rR[1] = rX[0] * r240['sin'] + rX[1] * r240['cos']

    left = [rL[0] + center[0], rL[1] + center[1]]
    right = [rR[0] + center[0], rR[1] + center[1]]
    return [left, right, C1]
```

Now, let's figure out how to rotate the triangle. If we're tiling the plane with triangles, the next triangle to the right and left will need to be flipped over. It will also need to be moved some distance from the previous triangle.

How does that work? It should be the same idea as earlier, when we rotated around our old point. We multiply and subtract from the sine and cosine of one another for the x and y axis:

```
# remember, we need to import this
from math import cos, sin

def rotate_points(toTurn, pivot, degrees):
    translate = [toTurn[0] - pivot[0], toTurn[1] - pivot[1]]
    # python's sine and cosine use radians instead of degrees
```

```
    rads = radians(degrees)
    ourCos = cos(rads)
    ourSin = sin(rads)

    x = translate[0] * ourCos - translate[1] * ourSin
    y = translate[0] * ourSin + translate[1] * ourCos

    # add back in the center point we move around
    return [x + pivot[0], y + pivot[1]]
```

Great. Let's try running that. Does it work?

If we pass each point in our triangle from before, we end up with the rotated triangle, with everything in its right place. It can help to try drawing two triangles to check that it's correct.

Checking our triangles are draw properly

Checking the Distance of Triangles

Now, let's figure out how to make the triangles the right distance from one another. They should align with no gaps and no overlaps.

Drawing the problem on a piece of graph paper can help. What does a perfect triangle look like, and what are its properties? How far away does one triangle need to be from the next triangle?

First, we need a new function to move our triangle, all at once. We now have two triangles: one right side up, and one upside down. With these two triangles, we should be able to tile across the entire screen. We just need a way of moving them to the right places.

So, let's add an x movement and a y movement to the points. A function to do this looks like this:

```
def translate_points(points, x, y):
    newArray = []
    for point in points:
        newArray.append([point[0] + x, point[1] + y])
    return newArray
```

This function takes in all the points in a triangle, and returns a new set of points at a new location.

So, how far away from each other do we need to move each of our triangles? Let's experiment and find out.

We'll start by taking the code for making our two triangles, and have them start from the zero point. That way, we can pass a set of offsets, and have the number of triangles we need to fill the screen get passed over.

We need to flip each of our triangles at their center, so we need the distance across our triangle at the center.

How do we get that?

Drawing Our Flipped Triangles in the Right Places

Look at our triangle. First, we can tell that all sides of our triangle should be the same length. Since each side has the same angle, this makes sense.

Is there a straightforward way to calculate the length of one of the sides? We can take the two bottom points and find the distance by subtracting one of the x positions from the other.

We could make sure to subtract the right side from the left side, in that order, or we could just ignore the potentially negative value, and use the absolute value of the distance.

Luckily, Python provides a method of obtaining the absolute value of a number, from the math library from which we got the cosine and sine functions earlier. The function is called **abs**, short for absolute value. It always returns a positive value, whether you send it a positive or negative number.

The code to import **abs** and get the distance of our triangle side looks like this:

```
from math import abs
triangy = create_rotated_triangle((screenWidth // 2, screenHeight // 2), T_SIZE, 0)

theDistance = abs(triangy[0][0] - triangy[1][0])
```

Because we're referring to the triangles as lists of lists, we'll need to keep track of where our first and second list variables end up on our triangle. Are they really our two bottom points?

Finally, we can put everything together and start performing our first tessellation. We'll create a single triangle, find it's line length, and then create a new, rotated triangle with a center point exactly one side length away from it.

The code looks something like this:

```
from math import abs
triangy = create_rotated_triangle((screenWidth // 2, screenHeight // 2), T_SIZE, 0)
initialShift = (screenWidth // 2 + abs(triangy[0][0] - triangy[1][0])  // 2,
    screenHeight // 2 - T_SIZE // 2)

theDistance =abs(triangy[0][0] - triangy[1][0])
triangyUpsidey = create_rotated_triangle(initialShift, T_SIZE, 180)

while running:
    screen.fill(black)

    pygame.draw.polygon(screen, red, triangy)
    pygame.draw.polygon(screen, yellow, triangyUpsidey)

    for event in pygame.event.get():
        if event.type == pygame.QUIT:
            running = False
    pygame.display.flip()
    clock.tick()
```

Running this will produce our two triangles right in the center.

Now all we need is to shift each one over, in a loop. The new loop we need looks like this:

```
while running:
    screen.fill(black)

    for i in range(15):
        for j in range(15):
           pygame.draw.polygon(screen, red, translate_points(triangy, theDistance *
                  i - 500, j *  76 - 500))
            pygame.draw.polygon(screen, yellow, translate_points(triangyUpsidey,
                  theDistance * i - 500, j * 76 - 500))

    for event in pygame.event.get():
        if event.type == pygame.QUIT:
            running = False
    pygame.display.flip()
    clock.tick()
```

But wait, how does that work?

Our first triangles were both in the center of the screen, and now we're shifting the first triangles to minus half the screen, so we start back over at the left-hand side of the screen. We then draw triangle by triangle, making the distance of 76 pixels between each center point of our triangles.

Running this code produces our first tessellated triangles, although they're not all that interesting just yet:

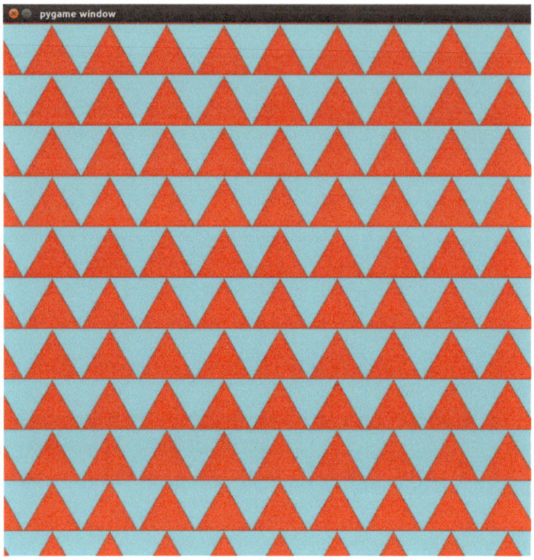

Making Our Tesselations More Interesting

Now, by playing around with our loop, we can start to create different tilings, and really start to see the various results we can get just by playing with what happens with our triangle spaces. For instance, try making the x or y distance between centerpoints longer than it needs to be. You can do this by changing the **76** that we multiplied by to **86**, creating a gap in our triangles.

This means we'll no longer have a gapless tessellation, but let's see what we can do:

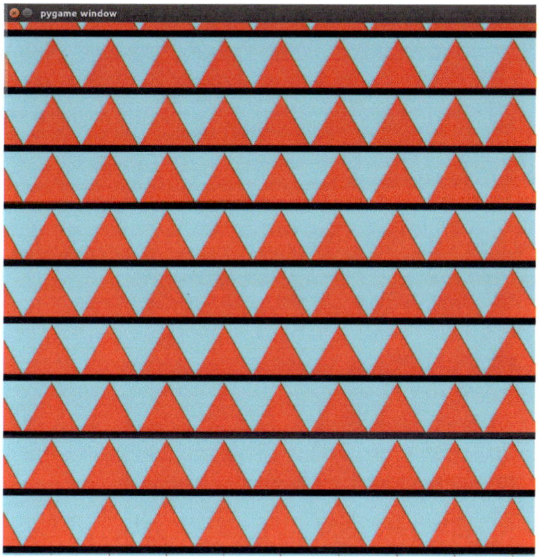

Or, try making the x or y smaller. You might also need to increase the range in both for loops to get the now smaller triangles to cover the entire screen:

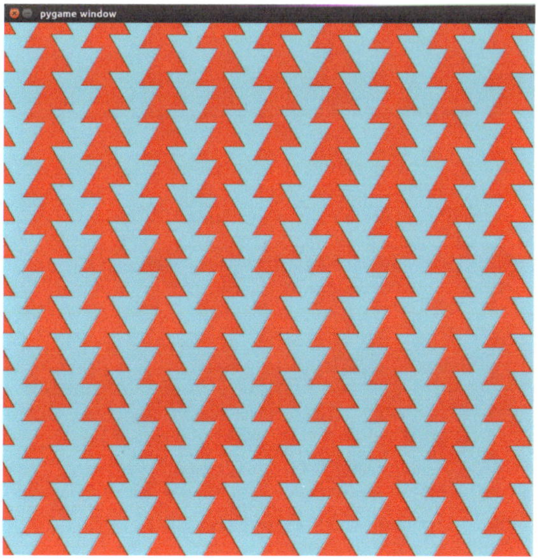

Even better, we can modify our code so that the distance between our centerpoints grows and shrinks as we move down the screen.

Something like this:

```
    for i in range(35):
        for j in range(35):
            pygame.draw.polygon(screen, red, translate_points(triangy, theDistance
                * i - 500, j *  100 - i - 500))
            pygame.draw.polygon(screen, yellow, translate_points(triangyUpsidey,
                theDistance * i - 500, j * 33 - 500))
```

...generates something totally new like this:

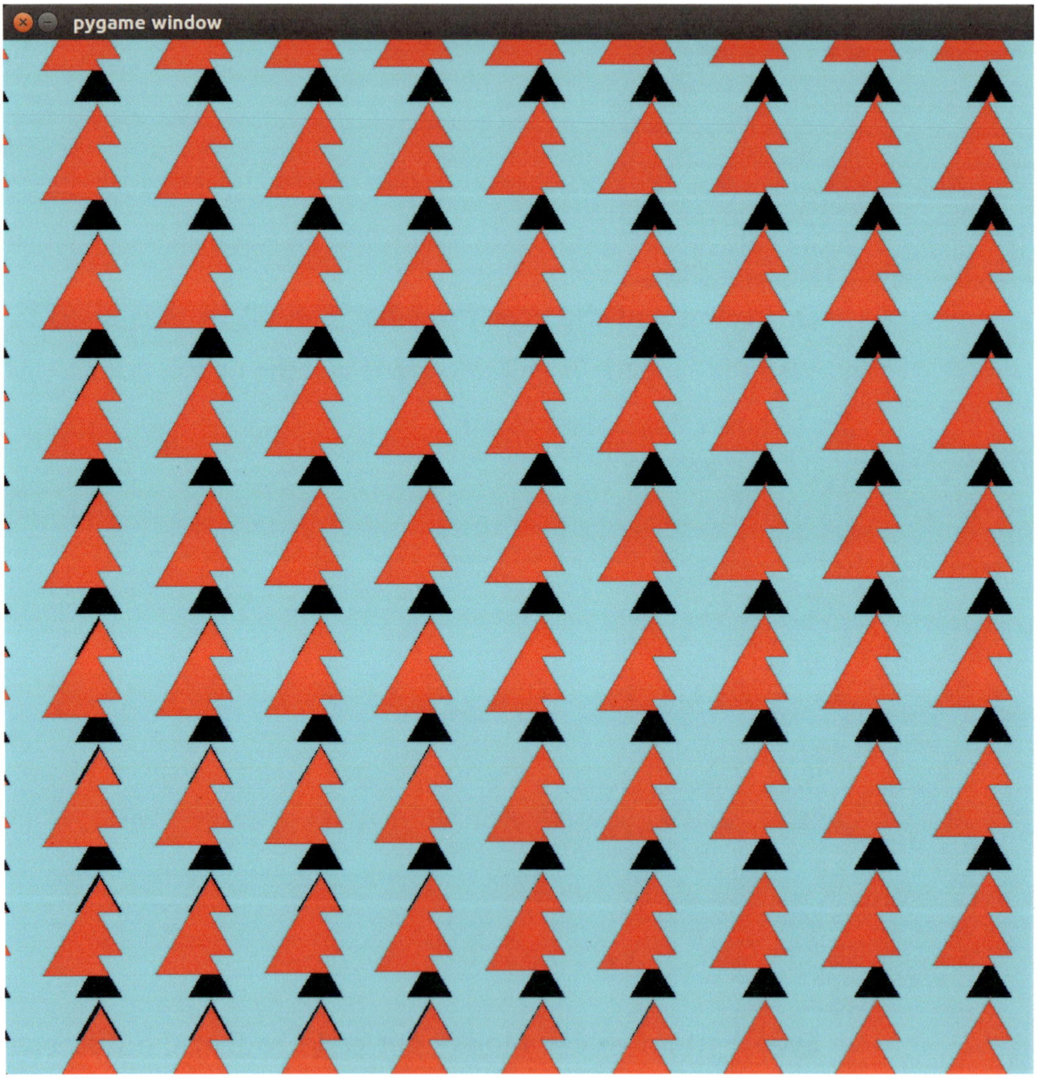

By building and understanding a new way of drawing across the entire screen, we've also given ourselves a totally new way of experimenting with other methods of drawing. With this technique, we can create our own, all-new tilings.

Tesselating Hexagons

Remember earlier, that we said we could also tile the plane with hexagons? Let's write the code for that.

The first thing to understand is how triangles tessellate into hexagons. If we look at a hexagon, how are they made up of triangles?

A hexagon comprises six triangles, one every 60 degrees, which adds up to a total of 360 degrees.

We'll need to create a centered triangle, and then spin it around the center point at each 60-degree angle. The code looks like this:

```
triangy = create_centered_triangle((screenWidth // 2, screenHeight // 2), T_SIZE)

for i in range(30, 360, 60):
    new = []
    for point in triangy:
        new.append(rotate_points(point, (screenWidth // 2, screenHeight // 2 - T_SIZE), i))
    other.append(new)
```

Now we have our first hexagon, so let's try drawing it on the screen:

```
while running:
    screen.fill(black)

    for i in other:
        pygame.draw.polygon(screen, red, i)
```

After running this code, we can see our first hexagon right there in the center of the screen:

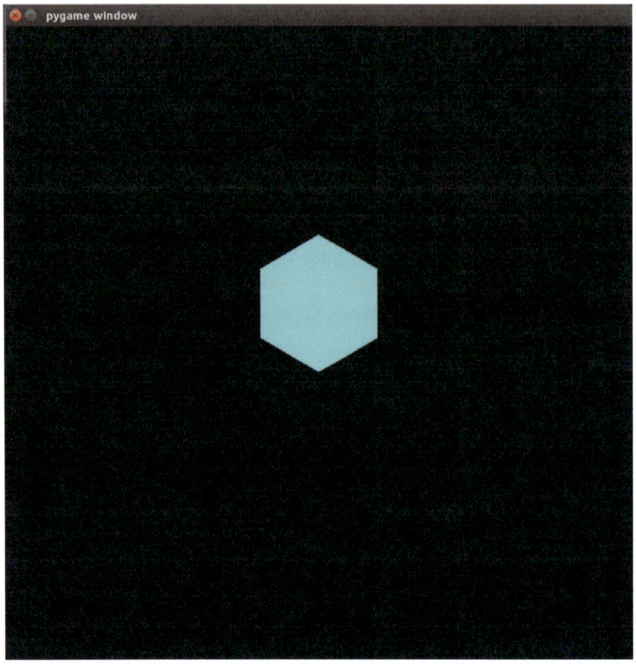

Now that we've got our first hexagon, we can colorize and rotate it so that it fits. Let's think through how the colors should be added, and then make a list to colorize it.


```
colors = [red, red, blue, blue, yellow, yellow]
```

Colorizing Our Hexagons

We need each color, two at a time, and we'll need to step through them in a list all over again. We can use our old friend, `enumerate`, to loop over the complete list of colors and end up with something we like:

```
for num, i in enumerate(other):
    pygame.draw.polygon(screen, colors[num], i)
```

Now we get our colored hexagon. Perfect!

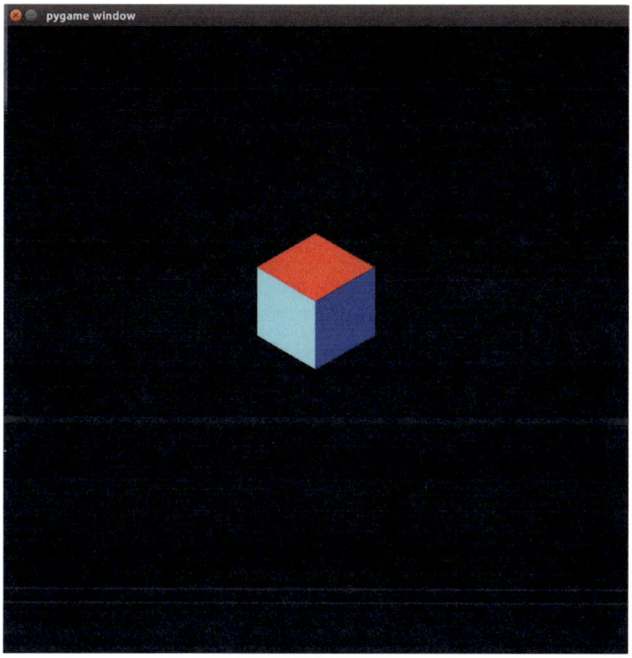

Next, let's make this thing tessellate, by making two lines, and alternating between the two. Each of our hexagons will need to be slightly offset from the other, and then, between the two of them, we should be able to tile the entire screen:

```
for i in range(10):
    for num, tri in enumerate(other):
        for a in range(10):
            moved = translate_points(tri, i * 150 - 650, a * 260 - 650)
            pygame.draw.polygon(screen, colors[num], moved)
            moved = translate_points(moved, 75, 130)
            pygame.draw.polygon(screen, colors[num], moved)
```

This gives us the tesselated hexagons we wanted:

But wait. Where did those numbers come from, by which we decided to move each of our hexagons?

Think about it. We know our hexagon is at least two triangle radiuses apart. So we try that. Then looking, visually, guess how much further we are after we run that code.

By doing this, we can get a feel for how the geometry we're building really works, and learn how to draw and invent the rules of our new geometry.

12
Inventing Interactive Tesselations

Another example tesselation

In this chapter, we'll write a program for inventing new tessellations.

We'll focus on the thought process of solving a complicated problem from scratch, when there's no direction for where to begin.

What does a programmer think about before writing code? Do they just jump right in? What problem do you solve first, when you're not even sure that a solution is possible?

Let's see if we can discover a way to start writing more sophisticated programs.

Survey the Problem Space

Before we even think about what our code might look like, let's first survey the space of custom tessellations. What sorts of tessellations are there, and are there any known rules for generating them?

A quick search turns up the grand master of custom tessellations, the artist M.C. Escher. He often uses fish and birds, and other things that blend seamlessly into one another.

But his drawings don't really seem to follow any logical set of rules, other than fitting shapes into one another like a jigsaw puzzle.

What is the most basic sort of a tessellation that we can customize? Perhaps something like the preceding image, with a deformed-square tessellation?

Discover the Rules

What's happening in the preceding image? We can see that there is some kind of repeating shape, but look at the image's corners. What's happening there? What rules can we see that make up this tessellation?

For one, there's a reflective change on both sides of the shape. If one side of the shape reaches out, the other side of the shape must reach in.

If we look at the base shape though, what sort of a tessellation is it? What most basic shape would add that deformation? It looks as if it began with a square tessellation, which means that we'll need to start with a square, and manipulate the shape to discover the rules that produce the final image.

Looking at the deformations applied to that initial square shape, we can see a mirror of the transformations on the opposite sides, for the top/bottom, and for the left/right sides.

Each deformation done on one side (either top/bottom, or left/right) must have the same transformation done to it in order to keep gaps from forming.

Draw It First

Now that we have an idea for what the rules might be (start with square, any point on the line can be moved, the same movement must happen on the corresponding side), let's try drawing out our own tessellations on paper to see if we can achieve the same effect. Let's also see if our hypotheseses are right about what the rules are for this tessellating universe.

We can start by trying out a new version of what we think our rules are, seeing if they apply, and then tessellating the plane. Grab a piece of grid paper, and measure along as we go.

If the rules fit, we can test and see whether there are any ways for our original rules to fail. If there is, it'll be much easier to fix now rather than later.

As I draw out different versions of my tessellation, I see the same things. My original rules were correct. Now, how do we allow the user to control them?

Make It Interactive

Suppose we were to make any mouse click change the shape of one side of our squares, and add the same change, inverted, to the opposite side. How could we make that happen?

We'd need to take the closest point on the square, relative to where the mouse was clicked on the screen, or we'd need to make our square's lines draggable. But that makes things much more difficult.

What if, instead, we give ourselves a few control points on each line? Can we get that to work?

With a list of control points, we can then shift over each line on each side of our square for its tessellations.

Making a Plan of Attack (For Code)

Now that we've surveyed the problem space, and we know the main pieces we'll need to put together, let's take a step back and think about what a logical process might look like to get our program running, step by step.

First, we need to draw a centered square. Then, we'll want to add our points, and then add our control points and distort the square, equally on both sides.

Finally, we can take our tessellatable shape, and duplicate it across the screen. To make it more visible, let's create it in two distinct colors, so we can easily see what we're doing.

Remember, it's always best to start with the smallest problem in front of you, and then bit by bit, inch your way closer to your goal.

Drawing a Square From Scratch

Let's start by writing a function for drawing the square. In this case, it's probably easiest to specify a center point, and a size for the square.

Again, it will help to draw it out on some grid paper:

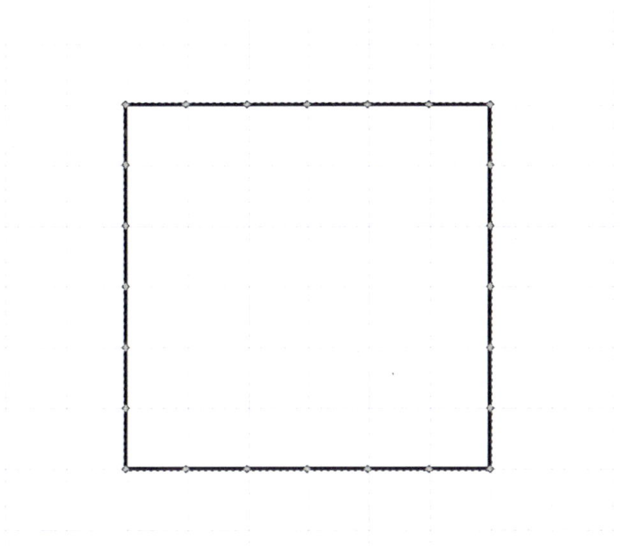

In this drawing, we can see that each corner is half the length away from the center point. So, we'll need to add or subtract half the length from the center point four separate ways:

```
def create_centered_square(length, centerPoint):
    hlength = length // 2
    topLeft = [centerPoint[0] - hlength, centerPoint[1] - hlength]
    topRight = [centerPoint[0] + hlength, centerPoint[1] - hlength]
    bottomLeft = [centerPoint[0] - hlength, centerPoint[1] + hlength]
    bottomRight = [centerPoint[0] + hlength, centerPoint[1] + hlength]

    # needs to be in proper drawing order for polygon to draw right
    return [topLeft, bottomLeft, bottomRight, topRight]
```

Great. Now, how would we add in our control points, to make the tessellation deformable? Could we add more points to the four points of our square?

Adding Midpoints To Our Square's Lines

Using the function we wrote previously, we can create another function to add midpoints to our square, for our click points. We should be smart about it, and use a points-per-line variable that lets us set how many points each side of the square should have:

```
def create_midpoints_square(length, centerPoint, pointsPerLine):
    base_square = create_centered_square(length, centerPoint)
    distance = length / pointsPerLine

    left, right, bottom, top = [], [], [], []
    for i in range(pointsPerLine):
        left.append([centerPoint[0] - length / 2, centerPoint[1] - length / 2
            + (i * distance)])
        right.append([centerPoint[0] + length / 2, centerPoint[1] + length / 2
            - (i * distance)])
        bottom.append([centerPoint[0] - length / 2 + (i * distance), centerPoint[1]
            + length / 2])
        top.append([centerPoint[0] + length / 2 - (i * distance), centerPoint[1] -
            length / 2])

    return left + bottom + right + top
```

We've wrapped our existing function with another one that divides the distance of every line into an equal amount of spaces.

So now we have our square, and we've got a set of points to manipulate it. But how do we add in the deformations; how do we deform our square?

Selecting A Point

Now we need a way of controlling all the deformation points, and we need to figure out how to get them to move in the appropriate direction, depending on where the user clicks.

We now have evenly spaced points in our square, and the next function should look through the list for the closest point to move when the mouse is clicked.

We also need to know how far the x and y coordinate of the click is from the old position in the square, so let's return that too. The rest of the program will rely on this, so let's write it now, and get it out of the way:

```
def find_index_of_closest(theList, thePoint):
    # First, we start with a really long distance
    lowest = 99999
    # Next, we keep track of the lowest place
    place = 0
    # Finally, we need to know how much the offset is
    xoffs, yoffs = 0, 0
    for m, point in enumerate(theList):
        # the measure of distance between two points
        distance = sqrt(pow(point[0] -  thePoint[0], 2) + pow(point[1] -
          thePoint[1], 2))
        if distance < lowest:
            place = m
            lowest = distance
            xoffs = thePoint[0] - point[0]
            yoffs = thePoint[1] - point[1]
    # Returns the place in the array, along with the offset
    return place, xoffs, yoffs
```

With this, we can start thinking about how to draw the mirror image on the other side of our square as we deform it. This can be difficult to think about clearly, so let's just start with the simplest of ideas: two lines.

If we move one point in the line by +15 in the x axis, how do we get the other side to do the same? We just add it. Easy enough.

But recall the fact that our square has a drawing order. When we pick a square number of points per side, we'll have to differentiate between vertical and horizontal lines, the top and bottom lines, and the left and right lines.

For our square's opposites to draw out properly, we'll need to think through how many points we'll have on our square, and how each line will end.

Let's ignore the corners. We don't want to end up distorting them, because doing so might make the whole drawing process more difficult. For example, we might end up making it so some of our drawing needs to be rotated.

Instead, let's just start with two controllable sides: the left side and the bottom side. By using these two sides as control points, we should be able to make the tessellations in real time and preview them in two different colors.

Finding the Opposite Point in the Square

To grab the opposite point in the square for tessellation, we'll need to return to our grid paper, and understand how the position of the opposite place in the square changes.

For our closest point on the first vertical line, let's add a number to each position, so we can see what the patterns might be.

```
def find_index_of_opposite(theList, thePlace):
    # add the duplicate corners, divide by four sides
    segmentLength = (len(theList) + 4) // 4

    if thePlace < segmentLength:
        return (segmentLength - 1) * 3 - thePlace
    elif thePlace < (segmentLength * 2):
        return (segmentLength - 1) * 4 - (thePlace - (segmentLength - 1))
```

With this code, we finally have a way to distort our square properly. Now it's time to start drawing the entire tessellation in one go.

Bringing It All Together to Draw

Now that we've got all the pieces built, let's bring them together and see how they work. We can worry about making the image tessellate after we make sure everything looks mostly right.

In this example, we set `SQUARE_SIZE` to 100, and the `LINE_POINTS` to 6. Try experimenting with these numbers to see how they change the way our tessellatable square changes.

Remember, only the left side and the bottom side of the square will be clickable. We'll click near a control point to have it jump to the mouse's position:

```
import pygame
import pygame.gfxdraw

pygame.init()

screenWidth, screenHeight = 800, 800
screenCenter = [screenWidth // 2, screenHeight // 2]

SQUARE_SIZE = 100
LINE_POINTS = 6

from math import sqrt # needed for distance calculation

screen = pygame.display.set_mode((screenWidth, screenHeight))

clock = pygame.time.Clock()

white = (255,255,255)
yellow = (0, 255, 255)
red = (255, 0 , 0)
blue = (0, 0, 255)
black = (0, 0, 0)

def rotate_point(toTurn, pivot, degrees):
    translate = [toTurn[0] - pivot[0], toTurn[1] - pivot[1]]
    rads = radians(degrees)
    ourCos = cos(rads)
    ourSin = sin(rads)
```

```
    x = translate[0] * ourCos - translate[1] * ourSin
    y = translate[0] * ourSin + translate[1] * ourCos

    return [x + pivot[0], y + pivot[1]]

def rotate_points(points, pivot, degrees):
    rotatedPoints = []
    for point in points:
        rotatedPoints.append(rotate_point(point, pivot, degrees))
    return rotatedPoints

def translate_points(points, dx, dy):
    newArray = []
    for point in points:
        newArray.append([point[0] + dx, point[1] + dy])
    return newArray

def create_centered_square(length, centerPoint):
    hlength = length // 2
    topLeft = [centerPoint[0] - hlength, centerPoint[1] - hlength]
    topRight = [centerPoint[0] + hlength, centerPoint[1] - hlength]
    bottomLeft = [centerPoint[0] - hlength, centerPoint[1] + hlength]
    bottomRight = [centerPoint[0] + hlength, centerPoint[1] + hlength]

    # needs to be in proper drawing order for polygon to draw right
    return [topLeft, bottomLeft, bottomRight, topRight]

def create_midpoints_square(length, centerPoint, pointsPerLine):
    base_square = create_centered_square(length, centerPoint)
    distance = length / pointsPerLine

    left, right, bottom, top = [], [], [], []
    for i in range(pointsPerLine):
        left.append([centerPoint[0] - length / 2, centerPoint[1] - length /
          2 + (i * distance)])
        right.append([centerPoint[0] + length / 2, centerPoint[1] + length /
          2 - (i * distance)])
        bottom.append([centerPoint[0] - length / 2 + (i * distance), center
          Point[1] + length / 2])
        top.append([centerPoint[0] + length / 2 - (i * distance), center
          Point[1] - length / 2])

    return left + bottom + right + top
```

```
def find_index_of_closest(theList, thePoint):
    lowest = 800
    place = 0
    xoffs, yoffs = 0, 0
    for m, point in enumerate(theList):
        distance = sqrt(pow(point[0] -  thePoint[0], 2) + pow(point[1] - thePoint[1], 2))
        if distance < lowest:
            place = m
            lowest = distance
            xoffs = thePoint[0] - point[0]
            yoffs = thePoint[1] - point[1]
    return place, xoffs, yoffs

def find_index_of_opposite(theList, thePlace):
    # add the duplicate corners, divide by four sides
    segmentLength = (len(theList) + 4) // 4

    if thePlace < segmentLength:
        return (segmentLength - 1) * 3 - thePlace
    elif thePlace < (segmentLength * 2):
        return (segmentLength - 1) * 4 - (thePlace - (segmentLength - 1))


def draw_flat_line(screen, x1, y1, length, color):
  for x in range(x1, x1 + length):
    pygame.gfxdraw.pixel(screen, x, y1, color)

def draw_vertical_line(screen, x1, y1, length, color):
  for y in range(y1, y1 + length):
    pygame.gfxdraw.pixel(screen, x1, y, color)

def draw_plus_sign(screen, x, y, size, color):
    draw_flat_line(screen, x - (size // 2), y, size, color)
    draw_vertical_line(screen, x, y - (size // 2), size, color)

running = True

theSquare = create_midpoints_square(SQUARE_SIZE, screenCenter, LINE_POINTS)

plusX, plusY = screenCenter

while running:
    screen.fill(black)

    pygame.draw.polygon(screen, yellow, theSquare)
```

```
    if pygame.mouse.get_focused():
      plusX, plusY = pygame.mouse.get_pos()

    draw_plus_sign(screen, plusX, plusY, 5, white)

    key = pygame.key.get_pressed()

    for event in pygame.event.get():
        # our mouse click gets checked here
        if event.type == pygame.MOUSEBUTTONDOWN:
            if event.button == 1: # left click
              place, xoffs, yoffs = find_index_of_closest(theSquare, [plusX, plusY])
                print("Index touched: %i" % place)
                print("xoffs: %i, yoffs: %i" % (xoffs, yoffs))

                if place in range(1, LINE_POINTS): # left line of square
                    opposite = find_index_of_opposite(theSquare, place)
                    theSquare[place] = [theSquare[place][0] + xoffs,
                       theSquare[place][1] + yoffs]
                    theSquare[opposite] = [theSquare[opposite][0] + xoffs,
                       theSquare[opposite][1] + yoffs]

                if place in range(LINE_POINTS + 1, LINE_POINTS * 2):
                       # bottom line of square
                    opposite = find_index_of_opposite(theSquare, place)
                    theSquare[place] = [theSquare[place][0] + xoffs,
                       theSquare[place][1] + yoffs]
                    theSquare[opposite] = [theSquare[opposite][0] + xoffs,
                       theSquare[opposite][1] + yoffs]


        if event.type == pygame.QUIT:
            running = False
    pygame.display.flip()
    clock.tick()
```

That's a lot of code! Let's walk through the setup and main loop, to make sure we understand what we've done to get this program running.

First, we create a midpoint square in the center of the screen using our **SQUARE_SIZE** variable and the number of **LINE_POINTS** we specify. Hopefully, you played with these values and saw how they can change the feel of the shapes we're creating.

Next, we get into our main loop, where we draw the polygon and check for the user's mouse clicks. By checking which element is closest to the user's mouse click, we can make sure the correct side gets moved in the right direction.

We use the `find_index_of_opposite` function to get the opposite point in the matrix, and then we add our x and y offsets from the other points' positions to add to the opposite side.

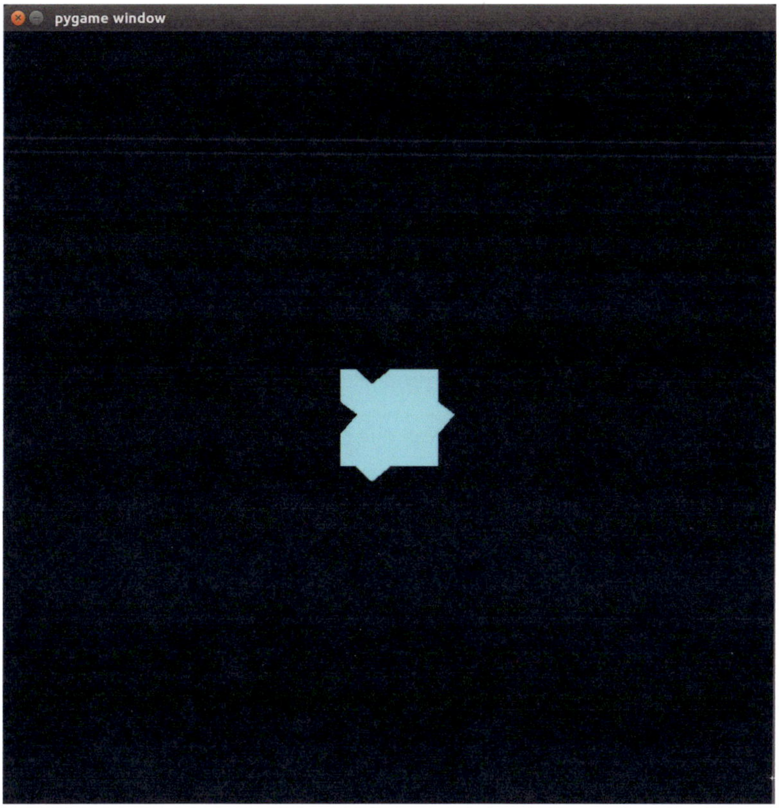

Now we're getting somewhere!

With our two if statements inside of our click event, we manage to do all the transformations necessary to draw our distortions as we click through the program. The only thing left to do now is tessellate this shape across the entire screen.

Tesselating Our New Shape

Now that we've got our shape created properly, let's figure out how we'd like to draw it across the screen.

We could just use a function to move the shape across the entire screen, and draw it over and over like we did in the previous chapter. But that's messy, so let's see if we can do better.

Let's try drawing our shape to two different surfaces and then copy those surfaces across the entire screen.

We'll need to create transparent surfaces, and then blit (or draw) them across our screen in the same size as our square's corners.

Note, though, that our top shape's distortions could be negative if we make the surface size the same as the square's original size. So, we'll need to make each side at least as long as our longest point in the square.

If you're confused, try getting rid of the `get_longest` in the code below for all the surface creations and point translations. You'll see how the top shape of the pieces gets cut off.

Finally, we'll want a control shape, so we can see where we're supposed to be clicking on the screen. Otherwise, we can just get lost in all the same patterns of shapes.

We'll use the `d` and `f` keys as before, to toggle on and off the drawing of a red version of our shape over the rest of the drawings we've done.

```
def get_longest(linePoints):
    longest = [0, 0]
    for i in linePoints:
        if abs(i[0]) > longest[0]:
            longest[0] = i[0]
        elif abs(i[1]) > longest[1]:
            longest[1] = i[1]
    return longest
```

```python

while running:
    screen.fill(black)
    surface1 = pygame.Surface((SQUARE_SIZE + get_longest(theSquare)[0] * 2,
                               SQUARE_SIZE + get_longest(theSquare)[1] * 2),
                                    flags=pygame.SRCALPHA)
    surface2 = pygame.Surface((SQUARE_SIZE + get_longest(theSquare)[0] * 2,
                               SQUARE_SIZE + get_longest(theSquare)[1] * 2),
                                    flags=pygame.SRCALPHA)

    pygame.draw.polygon(surface1, yellow,
                        translate_points(theSquare,
                                         get_longest(theSquare)[0],
                                         get_longest(theSquare)[1]))
    pygame.draw.polygon(surface2, blue,
                        translate_points(theSquare,
                                         get_longest(theSquare)[0],
                                         get_longest(theSquare)[1]))

    for i in range(15):
        for j in range(15):
            if i % 2 == 0:
                if j % 2 == 0:
                    screen.blit(surface1, (SQUARE_SIZE * i - OFFSCREEN, j *
                       SQUARE_SIZE - OFFSCREEN))
                else:
                    screen.blit(surface2, (SQUARE_SIZE * i - OFFSCREEN, j *
                       SQUARE_SIZE - OFFSCREEN))
            else:
                if j % 2 == 0:
                    screen.blit(surface2, (SQUARE_SIZE * i - OFFSCREEN,  j *
                       SQUARE_SIZE - OFFSCREEN))
                else:
                    screen.blit(surface1, (SQUARE_SIZE * i - OFFSCREEN,  j *
                       SQUARE_SIZE - OFFSCREEN))

    if pygame.mouse.get_focused():
      plusX, plusY = pygame.mouse.get_pos()

    draw_plus_sign(screen, plusX, plusY, 5, white)
    if drawMain:
       pygame.draw.polygon(screen, red, translate_points(theSquare, SQUARE_SIZE
          * 5 - 200,  5 * SQUARE_SIZE - 200))

    key = pygame.key.get_pressed()
```

```
    if key[pygame.K_d]:
        drawMain = False

    if key[pygame.K_f]:
        drawMain = True

    for event in pygame.event.get():
        # our mouse click gets checked here
        if event.type == pygame.MOUSEBUTTONDOWN:
            if event.button == 1: # left click
             place, xoffs, yoffs = find_index_of_closest(translate_points(theSquare,
                 SQUARE_SIZE * 5 - 200,
                 5 * SQUARE_SIZE - 200),
                                                                 [plusX, plusY])
                print("Index touched: %i" % place)
                print("xoffs: %i, yoffs: %i" % (xoffs, yoffs))

                if place in range(1, LINE_POINTS):
                    opposite = find_index_of_opposite(theSquare, place)
                    theSquare[place] = [theSquare[place][0] + xoffs,
                       theSquare[place][1] + yoffs]
                    theSquare[opposite] = [theSquare[opposite][0] + xoffs,
                       theSquare[opposite][1] + yoffs]

                if place in range(LINE_POINTS + 1, LINE_POINTS * 2):
                    opposite = find_index_of_opposite(theSquare, place)
                    theSquare[place] = [theSquare[place][0] + xoffs,
                       theSquare[place][1] + yoffs]
                    theSquare[opposite] = [theSquare[opposite][0] + xoffs,
                       theSquare[opposite][1] + yoffs]


        if event.type == pygame.QUIT:
            running = False
    pygame.display.flip()
    clock.tick()
```

Once we run this code, we finally have a full, 100% transformable, deformable tessellation.

A New Universe of Tesselations

This is an entire universe to play with, and we built it all from scratch!

13

Exporting Our Tesselations for Print

Ready for printing

The goal of this chapter is to get a decent-looking printout from our tessellation generator. For now, we have a low-resolution tool for making and playing with these tessellations, but we don't have a real way of exporting them for laser cutting, 3D printing, painting, and so on. In this chapter, we'll add that capability to what we've already built.

The first thing we'll do is add a keyboard shortcut to save a pickle of our drawing object from the previous example. Let's do that now, in the while loop:

```
if key[pygame.K_s]:
        import pickle
        pickle.dump(theSquare, open('out.pkl', 'wb'))
```

Rendering Vector Graphics

The preceding code gives us a file we can use to render a final drawing. Instead of a low-resolution drawing, at the end of this export process we'll have what's called a vector drawing—an image that can be scaled infinitely without losing detail.

We'll do this using a library for vector graphics, called "PyX."

Remember, you'll need to use the pip command to install PyX before you can start playing with the code that follows. (Install with a `pip install pyx` on the command line.)

Once you've saved your first export of a tessellation, try exploring the PyX library in an IPython shell using some of the example code from their site (http://pyx.sourceforge.net/examples/index.html).

For example, we might start with a simple line-drawing function call, just as is used for our current program. Looking at one of the example programs for PyX, it looks like it has this weird syntax:

```
from pyx import *

unit.set(wscale=10)

c = canvas.canvas()

c.stroke(path.line(2, 0, 3, 0) <<
         path.line(3, 0, 3, 1) <<
         path.line(3, 1, 2, 1) <<
         path.line(2, 1, 2, 0))

p = path.line(4, 0, 5, 0) << path.line(5, 0, 5, 1) << path.line(5, 1, 4, 1)
p.append(path.closepath())
c.stroke(p)

c.writePDFfile("addjoin")
```

What are those << markers, and what do they do? More importantly, how would we put them in our loop, going over each of the points in our tessellatable object?

Let's start by creating an IPython shell and exploring the example program with some slight changes:

```
$ ipython
Python 3.4.3+ (default, Oct 14 2015, 16:03:50)
Type "copyright", "credits" or "license" for more information.

IPython 4.0.3 -- An enhanced Interactive Python.
?          -> Introduction and overview of IPython's features.
%quickref -> Quick reference.
help       -> Python's own help system.
object?    -> Details about 'object', use 'object??' for extra details.

In [1]: import pyx

In [2]: p = pyx.path.line(0,0,1,1) << pyx.path.line(1,1,2,3)

In [3]: p
Out[3]: <pyx.path.path at 0x7fad75993ac8>

In [4]: p.path
Out[4]: <bound method path.path of <pyx.path.path object at 0x7fad75993ac8>>

```

```
In [5]: p.pathitems
Out[5]:
[<pyx.path.moveto_pt at 0x7fad759988b8>,
 <pyx.path.lineto_pt at 0x7fad75998948>,
 <pyx.path.lineto_pt at 0x7fad75998990>]
```

Aha! So, when we're using the `<<` command, what we're really doing is adding a `lineto_pt` to the `pathitems` array. For our tessellation to be drawn properly, we'll need to start with a point, and then append `lineto_pt` to the first line.

What does that look like? Let's continue with our IPython shell, and see if we can get something to output:

```
In [6]: pyx.path.lineto?
Init signature: pyx.path.lineto(self, x, y)
Docstring:      Append straight line to (x, y)
File:           /usr/local/lib/python3.4/dist-packages/pyx/path.py
Type:           type

In [7]: pyx.path.lineto_pt?
Init signature: pyx.path.lineto_pt(self, x_pt, y_pt)
Docstring:      Append straight line to (x_pt, y_pt) (coordinates in pts)
File:           /usr/local/lib/python3.4/dist-packages/pyx/path.py
Type:           type
```

OK, so it looks like we'll really need to just append `pyx.path.lineto` to each of the points in our shapes for tessellation. Our first attempt of that code might look like this:

```
from pyx import *
import pickle
unit.set(wscale=1000)

doubleArray = pickle.load(open('out.pkl', 'rb'))
print(doubleArray)
c = canvas.canvas()

p = path.line(doubleArray[0][0], doubleArray[0][1], doubleArray[1][0], doubleArray[1][1])
for place, point in enumerate(doubleArray):
    if place == 0 or place == 1:
        continue
    p.pathitems.append(path.lineto(doubleArray[place][0], doubleArray[place][1]))
```

```

p.append(path.closepath())
print(p)
c.stroke(p)
c.writePDFfile("addjoin")
c.writeSVGFile("addjoin")
```

One thing you might notice after trying the PyX library is that it doesn't follow the naming conventions we saw with Pygame, or even with what we've done so far. It doesn't stick with uppercase letters after the first word as we've been doing. You can see this in `c.writeSVGfile`, so be careful.

This code almost works, successfully printing out a shape, but it has one big problem. PyX is using a different x and y axis than our screen. We'll need to go back and mirror-flip our tessellation horizontally to make sure they match.

Adjusting Our Tesselation's Thickness

Another problem is that our tessellations look far too thick. We'll need to figure out how sizing works in our vector image, and then get the images to tessellate.

Let's look at the documentation for PyX. In it, we can find a way to specify how to change or set a color for a stroke. It looks something like this:

```
c.stroke(p, [trafo.mirror(180), style.linewidth.THIN])
```

It seems that stroke takes a list, filled with the transformations we want to make on that stroke. Even more interesting, when we get in an IPython shell and look to see what other options we have for linewidth, we see things like:

THin, THIn, Thin, thin

What could this mean?

his is one of those times where experimenting can help. Try running the program with each of these options, and you should see that the more letters that are capitalized, the thinner the lines become.

Next, let's tessellate our properly stroked shape across the screen. We'll do that by first creating a new canvas onto which to paste everything. We'll then create two for loops, one for the x and one for the y tessellation as far across as we want our tessellation to reach. Finally, we'll translate (or move) the shape as we draw across the screen. The code will eventually end up something like this:

```
cc = canvas.canvas()
for i in range(10):
    for j in range(10):
        cc.insert(c, [trafo.translate(i * 100, j * 100)])
```

After putting it all together and adding a new save for our new canvas, our application can now finally load up and turn each of our drawings into a single tessellatable shape, ready for printing. Try it with a drawing yourself, and see how well it prints.

We've added a bunch of new functionality to our program, and now we could take any of these files and resize them for printing. Or we could use the vector drawings themselves to machine-tool with CNC and cut them into real-life pieces of wood or plastic.

In Pygame, we were writing to a screen. With PyX, we're writing to a canvas via a line series, and that line series can be modified with a set of transformations and made into a stroked line or a colored shape.

Starting from here, we can start to see how linking together separate libraries gives us a completely new way to approach building our programs. As our ideas for programs get bigger and more complex, we can write little sketch programs of portions of the problems.

We can then link them together, using our basic Python objects as the "glue."

Indeed, this is the way a lot of programming works in general. First you research and try to figure out what problem you're trying to solve. Then, you discover what existing tools you can reuse, and how those tools can be used in combination with other things that already exist. By bringing the two different things together, you start to create something completely new.

Creating Glitches in Our Tessellations

Now that we have a way of building our tessellations, and a method of printing them out, let's "break" our seamless tessellations and see if we can make something else interesting out of what we have.

Let's bring back in our rotation functions, `rotate_point` and `rotate_points`, from earlier, and then run them through the code we just wrote. These functions don't need to be modified at all.

Next, let's return to the code just outside our `for` loop and change how we create our square for drawing:

```
theSquare = create_midpoints_square(SQUARE_SIZE, (SQUARE_SIZE // 2, SQUARE_SIZE
    // 2), LINE_POINTS)

theSquare = rotate_points(theSquare, (SQUARE_SIZE // 2, SQUARE_SIZE // 2), 45)
plusX, plusY = screenCenter

SQUARE_SIZE = 80
```

We create our square as before, and then we rotate our new square around its center by 45 degrees. This gives us rotated squares aligned diagonally.

Changing the `SQUARE_SIZE` creates more or less space between the squares when we draw. Try running the program with these changes and see what you get.

To produce three colors for the tessellations, try setting `SQUARE_SIZE` to `145`. As long as your original square is 100 pixels wide, you should now have three diagonal colors with which to draw. (Remember, the third color comes from the background of your drawing itself, so you'll need to change the background color to get a new image.)

SQUARE_SIZE set to 145 gives us equal distance

By playing with the distance between the squares, we can create different glitches (or digital imperfections) for our tessellations, perhaps breaking them a bit, but giving us newer ideas to use.

By changing the distances in our `drawPyx` draw function, we can reach a point where we create slightly glitched drawings.

By changing the loop in the previous `drawPyx` to half the distance between our drawing before, we end up with the following code, and the following output:

```
cc = canvas.canvas()
for i in range(10):
    for j in range(10):
        cc.insert(c, [trafo.translate(i * 73, j * 73)])
```

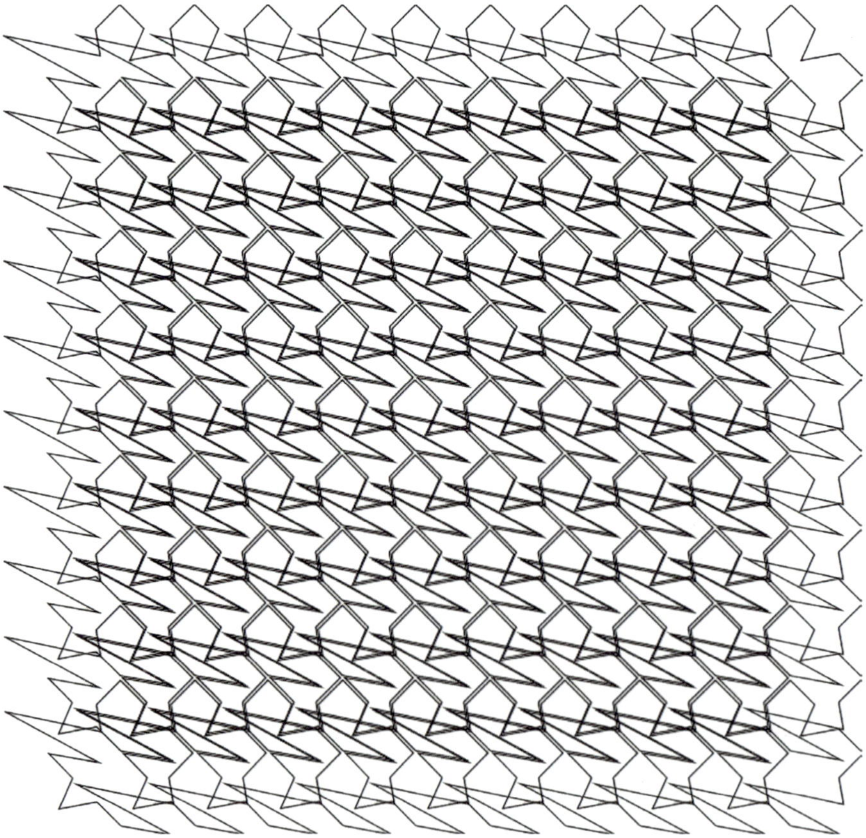

Previous image exported at half distance

Now, let's add some color to make that export look better.

Colorizing our Tesselations with Inkscape

Now that we have vector graphics, we can import them into a vector graphics program, where we can edit, color, and export the graphics for printing, CNC cutting, 3D printing, or anything else we like.

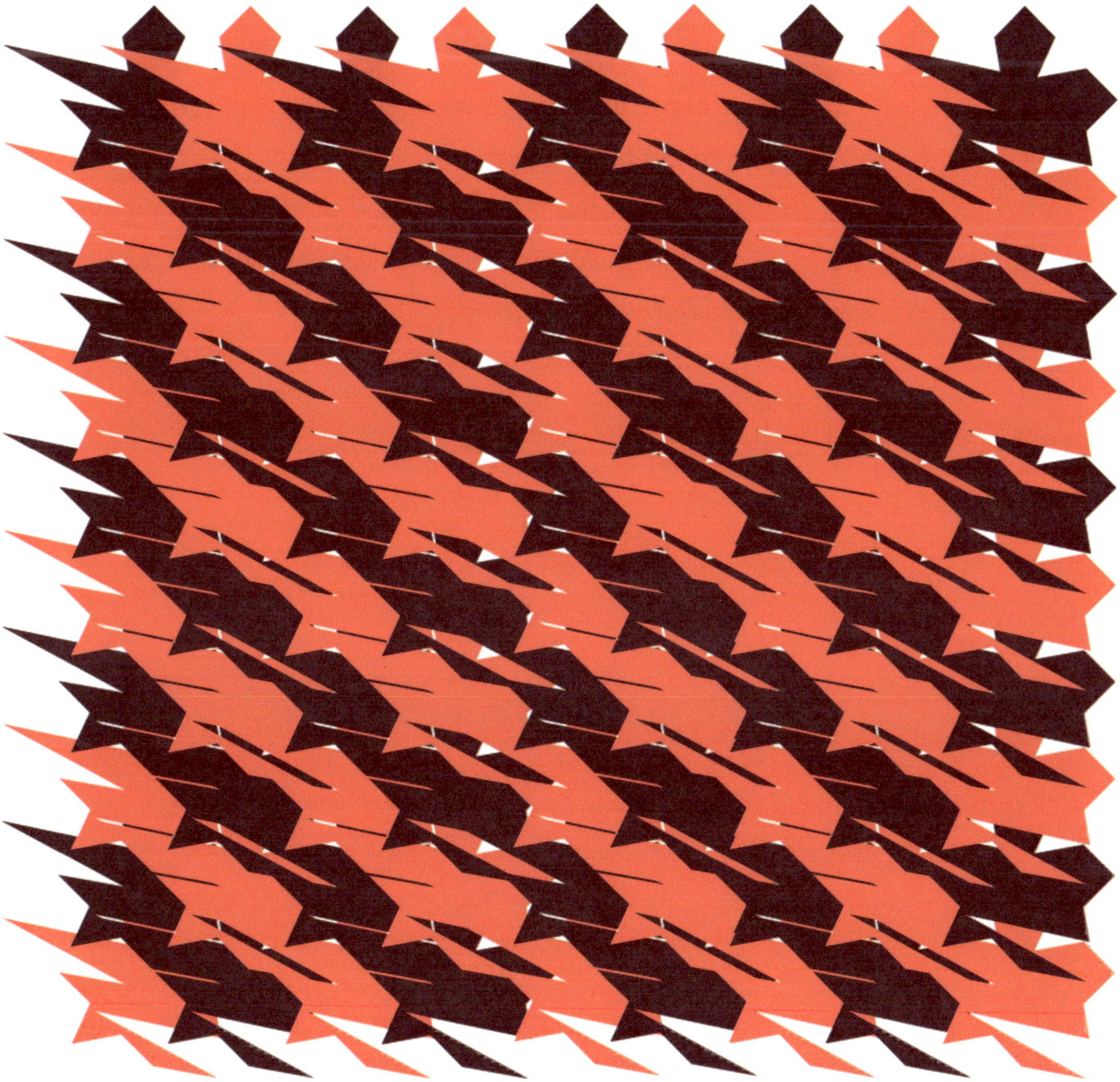

Colorizing based upon the same pattern

Using Inkscape, we can make all the sorts of vector image changes we can imagine. Let's try importing the PDF file that we saved earlier, and see how we can manipulate our exported graphics to display in new ways.

Again, if you're running Ubuntu Linux, installing Inkscape is easy with a `sudo apt-get install inkscape`. Windows and Mac versions should have their own instructions on the Inkscape page (https://inkscape.org/).

When we open our PDF in Inkscape, we're greeted with a thin outline of our drawing. By pressing Ctrl+A, we can grab all the instances of our tessellation.

If we open up the Fill and Stroke dialog by pressing Ctrl+Shift+F, we can then select either a gradient or a color for both our tessellation and its outline.

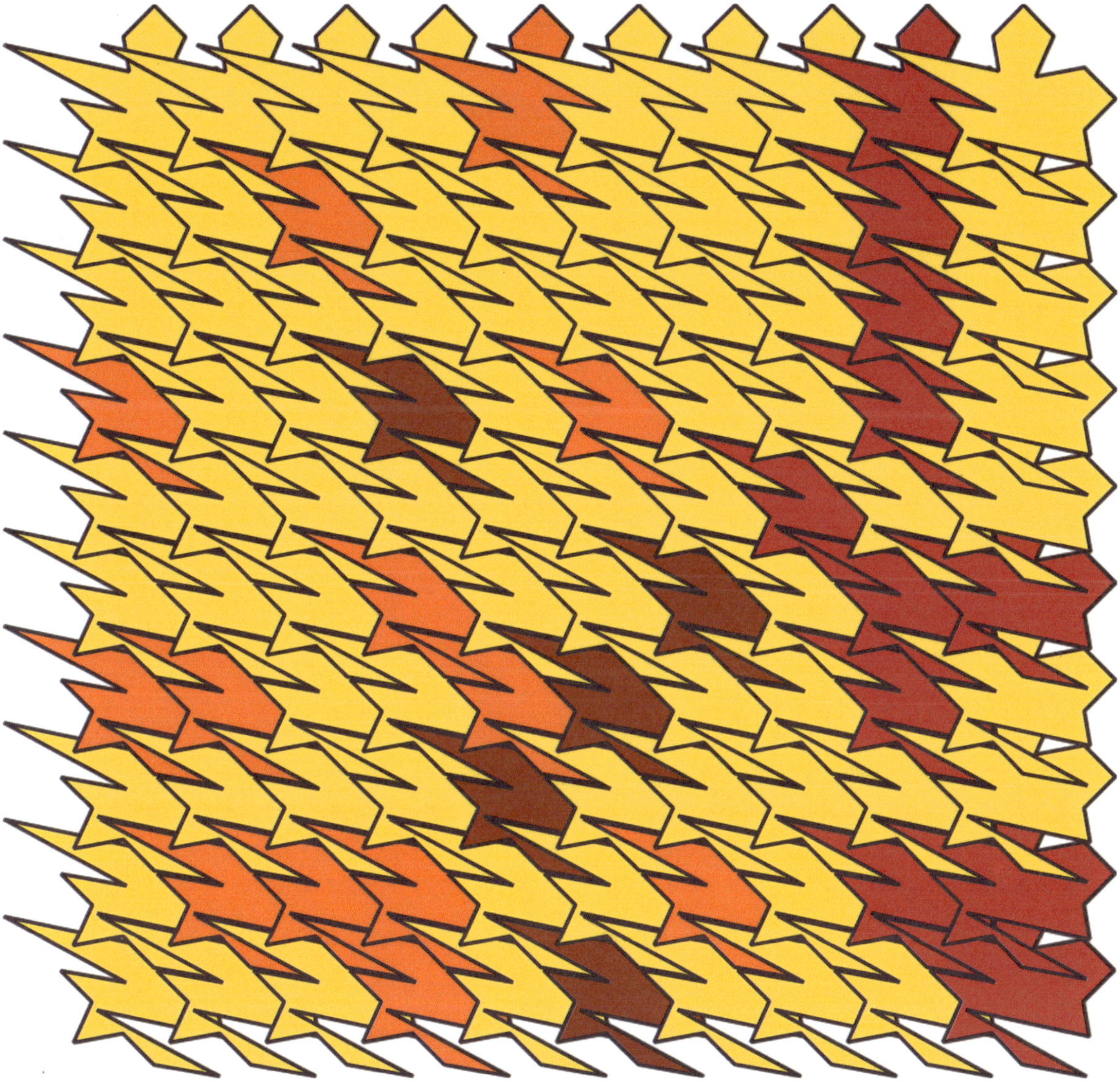

Randomly selecting and changing colors in our tesselation

Try experimenting with all the tools in Inkscape. You can move your tessellations across the screen, fill different portions with unique colors, and then save it out.

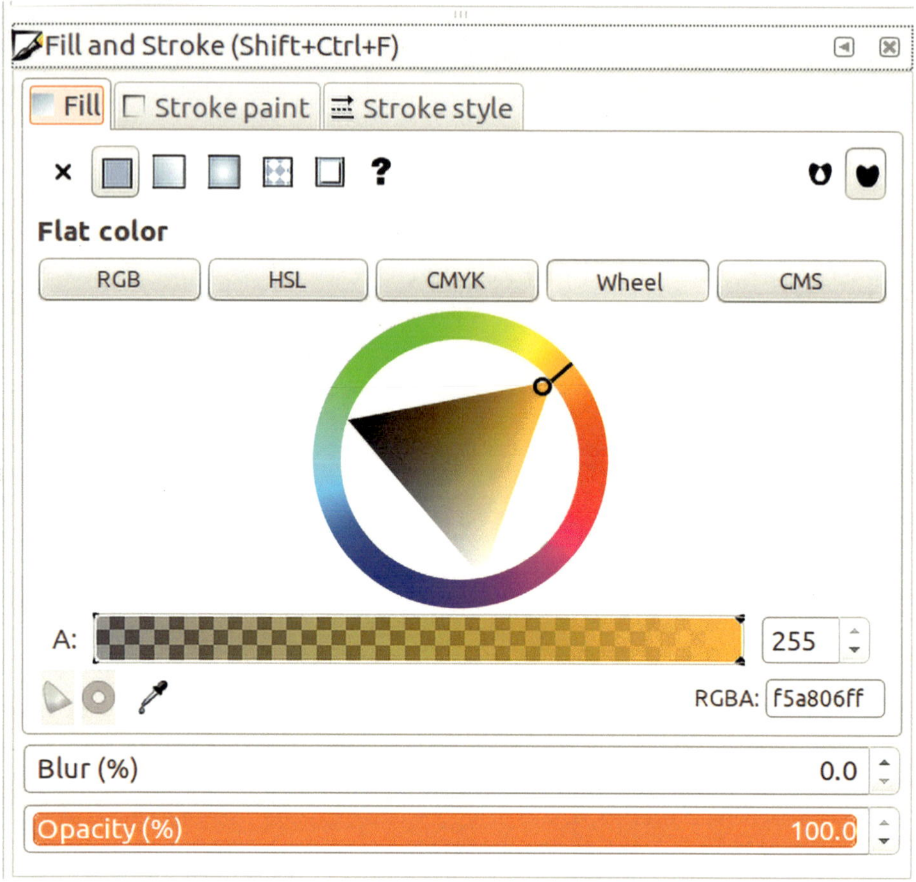

Choose our stroke color and opacity to change our tesselations

Once we're finished, we can export our vector graphics image to print as large as we like. (Recall that vector images won't lose detail when resized, and can be scaled to as large or small as we like, without losing any fidelity.)

Exploring Further

With our final edits in Inkscape, we've taken an idea, implemented it in software, exported it for editing, and then brought it to finished form, ready for printing at any size.

With this final process, we've come full circle with our development process. We're now able to take ideas and transform them into unique new tools for expressing ourselves and exploring new ideas.

We don't work from scratch; we incorporate the efforts other people have made. But by adding our own ideas, we take those efforts even further.

Where to go from here? Which project along the way spoke to you the most—reached out to you the loudest? We could start making interactive graphics programs that glitch our images even further, or we could make new vector images, or we can just continue to play with shapes further.

Each piece along the way affects everyone differently. I hope that you found something that spoke to you in this book—something that you'd like to take further and make your own.

Programming is a solitary endeavor, but sharing our process, and borrowing and contributing new ideas, is what makes it so exciting. With your first program, you can start contributing your own unique voice to shape the future.

I hope to see your work soon!

Made in United States
Troutdale, OR
11/11/2026

57125327R00112